Senior's Gmail Companion

An Effortless and Updated Guide to Using Gmail the Easy Way—Even If You're Not Tech-Savvy

CHITTAH PUBLISHING

Disclaimer

This book is intended to provide helpful and practical information about using Gmail, particularly for seniors or individuals who may not be familiar with digital technology. Every effort has been made to ensure the accuracy and completeness of the content at the time of publication.

However, Gmail is a service owned and operated by Google, Inc., and updates or changes to its platform may occur after this book is published. The author and publisher are not affiliated with Google, nor do they claim any endorsement or sponsorship from Google.

This guide does not provide technical support or personalized troubleshooting services. Users are encouraged to consult the official Google Help Center or seek professional assistance if needed.

Use of the information provided in this book is at your own discretion and risk. The author and publisher shall not be held liable for any damages or issues arising from the use of this material.

Table Of Contents

TABLE OF CONTENTS 2

CHAPTER 1: GETTING STARTED...6

What Is Gmail? 6

Why Gmail Is Great for Seniors 8

What You Need to Get Started 12

Creating a Google Account Step-by-Step 16

Signing Into Gmail for the First Time 21

CHAPTER 2: EXPLORING THE GMAIL INTERFACE 26

The Inbox: Tabs and Sections Explained................................26

Menu Bar and Icons 30

What Do All the Buttons Do? (Archive, Trash, Spam, etc.) 35

What Do All the Buttons Do? (Archive, Trash, Spam, etc.) 41

CHAPTER 3: SENDING AND RECEIVING EMAILS 48

How to Compose a New Email 48

Adding an Attachment (Photo or File) 52

Replying and Forwarding Emails 56

Using CC and BCC...61

Sending Group Emails 66

CHAPTER 4: STAYING ORGANIZED..72

Labels vs. Folders: What's the Difference?.............................72

Creating Folders for Friends, Family, Doctors, etc. 76

▯ Archiving vs. Deleting Emails..80

🔍 Using the Search Bar to Find Old Emails...85

⬡ Recognizing Spam and Phishing Emails...89

🛡 What to Do With Suspicious Emails..90

🔒 Setting a Strong Password..90

🔐 Enabling 2-Step Verification...91

📝 Reporting Scams..92

CHAPTER 6: CUSTOMIZING GMAIL FOR YOUR COMFORT.......................................94

Adjusting Font Size and Layout..94

📬 Adding an Email Signature in Gmail...97

📬 Adding an Email Signature in Gmail...100

🔔 Notifications: Turning Alerts On or Off..103

📱 How to Manage Notifications on Your Phone or Tablet...104

🖥 How to Manage Notifications on Your Computer (Web Browser)..............................104

CHAPTER 7: GMAIL ON MOBILE DEVICES..108

Installing the Gmail App (Android/iPhone)..108

📲 Signing In and Using Gmail on Phones or Tablets...110

📷 Sending Photos from Your Phone..113

▢📱 Managing Emails on the Go..116

CHAPTER 8: CONTACTS AND GROUPS...120

🗂 Adding and Saving New Contacts..120

✂ Editing or Deleting Contacts...121

👥 Creating Contact Groups (for Family, Church, Clubs, etc.)....................................122

CHAPTER 9: TROUBLESHOOTING AND HELP..126

🔑 Forgot Your Password? Here's What to Do 126

⚙️ Gmail Running Slow? Quick Fixes 127

📞 How to Reach Google Support 129

📓 Helpful Resources for Continued Learning 130

❋ Final Thoughts 131

💡 Before You Dive In

If this book ends up being helpful, please consider leaving a quick review on Amazon. It only takes a minute, but it helps others, especially fellow seniors, find the support they need too. 👥

Chapter 1: Getting Started

 What Is Gmail?

Let's start right at the beginning.

Imagine your mailbox at the front of your house. Now picture that mailbox on your computer or phone—only smarter, faster, and much safer. That's **Gmail** in a nutshell!

Gmail (short for *Google Mail*) is a free email service that lets you send and receive messages—just like letters, but instantly. You can use it to:

- Write to family and friends
- Receive appointment reminders
- Send photos of your grandkids
- Get updates from your doctor or church
- Shop online and receive order confirmations

And the best part? You can do it **anytime, anywhere**, from any device connected to the internet.

So, What Exactly Is an Email?

An email (electronic mail) is a message you send over the internet. Just like mailing a letter, each email has:

- A **To** address (who you're writing to)
- A **Subject** line (what it's about)
- A **Message** (what you want to say)

And instead of waiting days for it to arrive—it gets there in seconds!

💡 Why Use Gmail Instead of Regular Mail?

Here are just a few reasons Gmail is worth learning:

✅ **It's Free.** No stamps, no envelopes—just type and send.

✅ **It's Instant.** Messages arrive within seconds.

✅ **It's Safe.** Gmail protects you from junk mail and scams.

✅ **It's Smart.** It automatically sorts your mail into folders like Inbox, Promotions, and Spam.

✅ **It's Connected.** You can use your Gmail address to sign up for other services like YouTube, Google Maps, and more.

✳️ Why Gmail Is Great for Seniors

Technology can sometimes feel overwhelming, especially when it's constantly changing. But not all technology is complicated—Gmail is one of the simplest tools you can learn, **and once you get comfortable with it, you'll wonder how you ever managed without it!**

Whether you're 60, 70, or 90 years young, Gmail was made with you in mind—**especially when you follow a guide like this one that's written in plain, friendly language.**

Let's talk about all the ways Gmail can truly make your life easier, safer, and more connected.

📩 1. Easy Communication with Loved Ones

Staying in touch has never been more important. With Gmail, you can:

- Send a message to your children or grandchildren—even if they live across the world.
- Receive photos, updates, and special announcements (like birthdays, school reports, or wedding invitations).
- Share your own updates, stories, or even a recipe with just a few clicks.

No more waiting for letters to arrive or dealing with hard-to-hear phone calls. Gmail lets you communicate instantly and clearly—anytime, anywhere.

2. Simple and Senior-Friendly Design

Gmail is clean and well-organized. It uses large, readable fonts and clear buttons like:

- **Inbox** – where your messages arrive
- **Compose** – to write a new email
- **Trash** – to delete unwanted messages
- **Spam** – where junk mail goes (so it doesn't bother you)

And if you find the text too small, you can **adjust the font size** easily. We'll show you how later in the book!

---

3. Safe and Secure (Your Protection Matters!)

One of the biggest fears people have about the internet is safety. And rightly so! But Gmail is built with **strong protection** features, including:

- **Spam Filters** – Gmail automatically keeps unwanted or dangerous messages away from your inbox.
- **Two-Step Verification** – This adds an extra layer of security, so only *you* can access your account.
- **Password Recovery Options** – If you forget your password (and it happens to everyone!), Gmail helps you reset it safely.

So yes—you can use Gmail with peace of mind.

---

4. Accessible on All Devices

Whether you prefer a desktop computer, laptop, tablet, or smartphone—Gmail works on all of them. You can:

- Check your email from your recliner

- Read messages while sipping coffee at your kitchen table
- Reply to a note while on vacation—without needing to carry paperwork

Even if you switch devices later, Gmail keeps everything **saved in one place**, ready for you to access.

⏳ 5. Saves Time and Keeps You Organized

Say goodbye to stacks of paper, lost letters, or forgotten notes. Gmail:

- **Stores all your messages in one place**
- **Allows you to search for a name, date, or word** to find an old email
- **Let's you set reminders or star important messages** so you can easily come back to them

It's like having a tidy personal assistant, helping you keep track of everything.

🛍️ 6. Great for Shopping and Appointments

These days, many services send updates through email:

- Doctor's offices send appointment confirmations and lab results
- Online stores send receipts and shipping notices
- Banks send alerts and monthly statements

With Gmail, you can manage all of these easily without going to the post office or waiting for paperwork in the mail.

🌐 7. One Account, Many Possibilities

Here's something even better: once you create a Gmail account, it opens the door to other helpful Google services like:

- **Google Calendar** – for tracking appointments
- **Google Photos** – for storing and sharing pictures
- **Google Maps** – for finding directions to places
- **YouTube** – for watching how-to videos, sermons, or music

It's all connected under one Gmail login. You don't need a bunch of passwords and usernames—just your Gmail and you're in!

😊 Final Thought: It's Never Too Late to Start

You might be thinking:

"Is this really something I can learn at my age?"

Yes, it absolutely is. Many seniors just like you are discovering how empowering it feels to use Gmail. And the more you use it, the easier it becomes.

Think of Gmail as a modern mailbox—**but smarter, safer, and always right at your fingertips.**

You're already doing something amazing by taking the time to learn. And don't worry— we'll guide you every step of the way.

🔧 What You Need to Get Started

Before you begin using Gmail, think of it like preparing to bake a cake. You don't need anything fancy—just a few simple ingredients. In this case, your "ingredients" are everyday items that most people already have, or can easily access. And don't worry—we'll go over each one clearly, step by step.

By the end of this section, you'll feel fully prepared to create and use your very own Gmail account with confidence.

🖥️ *1. A Device: Your Gateway to the Internet*

To use Gmail, you'll need a **device** that connects to the internet. Here are your options:

📱 *Smartphone*

This is one of the most popular ways seniors use Gmail today.

- If you have a smartphone (like an iPhone or Android), you can download the Gmail app and check your email on the go.
- Touchscreen, easy to hold, and perfect for short messages and photos.

💻 *Computer or Laptop*

- Ideal if you're more comfortable with a larger screen and keyboard.
- You can visit the Gmail website using your web browser (like Google Chrome or Safari).

📱 *Tablet or iPad*

- Bigger than a phone but smaller than a laptop.
- Combines the ease of touch with a clear, larger display.

Tip: If you don't have a device yet and are looking to buy one, many local stores can help you choose something user-friendly, affordable, and senior-friendly. Ask a family member or store associate to guide you toward a simple model.

---

2. A Working Internet Connection

Next, you'll need to be connected to the internet. Without it, Gmail can't send or receive messages.

How Do I Get Internet?

- If you have Wi-Fi at home, great! You're already set.
- If not, consider contacting a local internet provider (or asking a family member) to help set it up.
- You can also access Gmail at places like:
    - A local library
    - Senior centers
    - Coffee shops with free Wi-Fi

Tip: Once you're connected, your device will usually remember the internet network, so you won't have to do this every time.

---

3. A Mobile Phone Number (For Security)

Gmail wants to make sure your account stays protected. That's why they ask for a **mobile phone number** when you sign up. Here's why it's important:

- You'll receive a **verification code** by text to confirm it's really you.
- If you forget your password in the future, Google can send a recovery code to your phone.

Don't worry—your phone number won't be shared publicly, and it won't be used to send you spam.

📝 4. A Notebook or Notepad (Yes, Really!)

This might sound old-fashioned, but it's one of the smartest things you can do.

Use a small **notebook** or even sticky notes to write down:

- Your **Gmail email address** (example: dorothy.smith@gmail.com)
- Your **password** (make it secure, but something you can remember)
- Your **backup phone number** or recovery details
- Any helpful notes you want to remember as you learn

💡 **Bonus Tip:** Keep this notebook somewhere safe but easy for you to find—like in a drawer near your computer or taped to the side of your desk.

☁ 5. A Willing Spirit and a Bit of Patience

You don't need to be a tech wizard. All you need is:

- A willingness to learn something new
- A little time to practice
- The courage to ask for help when you need it (and that's totally okay!)

Nobody becomes an expert in one day. But with this guide, you'll get there one step at a time—and you'll never be alone on the journey.

👓 Optional But Helpful

These aren't required but can make things easier:

- **Reading glasses** if your screen text looks small
- A **stylus pen** if you're using a touchscreen and prefer not to use your fingers

- A **comfortable chair and quiet space**, so you can concentrate while learning

---

✔ Quick Checklist: Do You Have Everything?

Here's a simple checklist to help you feel ready:

✔	Item
☐	A device (phone, computer, or tablet)
☐	A stable internet connection
☐	A mobile phone number
☐	A pen and notebook
☐	A calm place and a curious mind

If you've checked off most of these, then you're ready for the next step!

▣ Creating a Google Account Step-by-Step

(A Simple Walkthrough for First-Time Users)

Before you can start using Gmail, you need a Google Account. **Think of it as your online key to unlock not only Gmail, but other useful tools like Google Maps, YouTube, Google Photos, and more—all with one username and password.**

But don't worry: creating a Google Account is easy, **and we'll guide you through it step by step, using plain language, simple instructions, and lots of encouragement.**

🕐 *Step 1: Open Your Internet Browser*

No matter what device you're using—smartphone, tablet, or computer—you'll begin by opening a browser.

- On most devices, look for icons like:
    - 🌐 **Google Chrome**
    - 🧭 **Safari** (on iPhones or iPads)
    - ⬛ **Microsoft Edge** or **Firefox**

🔍 **Once it's open**, type this into the address bar at the top of the screen:

```
CopyEdit
www.gmail.com
```

Then press **Enter** or tap the "Go" or "Search" button.

✍ Step 2: Click "Create Account"

Once the Gmail page loads, you'll see a sign-in box. But since you're new, look for and click the link that says:

"Create account"

✅ Choose the option:

"For myself" (unless you're creating it for a business or someone else)

😎 Step 3: Enter Your Basic Information

Now it's time to tell Google a little about yourself. You'll see a form that asks for:

- **First Name** (e.g., Mary)
- **Last Name** (e.g., Johnson)
- **Username** (this will become your email address, like mary.johnson@gmail.com)
  - If your name is already taken, try adding numbers like `mary.johnson1954` or `mary. johnson22`
- **Password** – Choose a password that's:
  - Easy for **you** to remember
  - Hard for others to guess
  - At least 8 characters, with a mix of letters and numbers (e.g., `ApplePie1954`)
- **Confirm Password** – Type it again to be sure you didn't make a typo

💡 **Write your email and password down in your notebook** as soon as you choose them.

📱 Step 4: Add a Phone Number (For Safety)

Google will ask for your **mobile number**. This is to help:

- Verify that you're a real person (not a robot)
- Send you a **security code**
- Help you **recover your account** if you ever forget your password

✅ Type in your phone number and click **Next**.

📤 You'll receive a **6-digit code by text message**.

🌐 **Tip:** If you don't receive it within a minute, check your signal or ask someone for help. Then enter the code in the space provided.

🎂 Step 5: Add Recovery Info & Birthday

Google may also ask for:

- **Recovery Email (optional):** If you have another email, you can list it here. It's okay to leave this blank if this is your first and only email.
- **Birthday:** Use your real date of birth. Google uses it to protect your account.
- **Gender:** Choose the option that fits you best.

Click **Next** to continue.

📄 Step 6: Review Privacy Terms

This part shows Google's privacy and terms of use.

📖 You don't have to read every word, but here's what's important:

- Your data is private
- You control what's shared

- Google uses your information to personalize your experience (like suggesting useful emails)

✅ Scroll down and click **"I Agree"** when you're ready.

🎉 Step 7: Welcome to Your New Gmail!

Ta-da! 🎊
You've just created your very first Gmail account!

You'll be taken straight to your **inbox**, which is like a digital mailbox where all your messages will appear. It might be empty now, but soon you'll be sending and receiving emails like a pro.

📔 Recap: What You've Accomplished

| ✅ | You opened your internet browser | | ✅ | You went to www.gmail.com | | ✅ | You clicked "Create account" and entered your details | | ✅ | You verified your phone number | | ✅ | You accepted Google's terms | | ✅ | You now have your very own Gmail address! |

👏 Pat yourself on the back—you just completed a major step toward becoming tech-savvy and connected.

🔧 Trouble Signing Up?

Here are a few quick solutions to common issues:

- **Didn't get the text code?** Try again or check your phone number.
- **Password not strong enough?** Try adding a symbol like ! or @.

- **Username already taken?** Try adding a number or middle name.

If you're ever stuck, ask a friend or relative for a quick hand—or come back to this guide. You're never too old to learn something new!

🍞 Signing Into Gmail for the First Time

(Your First Step Into the World of Email)

Now that you've created your very own Gmail account—congratulations again! 🎉 — it's time to learn how to sign in **and** access your inbox.

Think of it like walking up to your personal digital mailbox. You have the key (your email and password), and now it's just about opening the door.

Whether you're using a computer, tablet, or smartphone, we're going to walk you through it step by step**, nice and slow.**

💻 *Option 1: Signing In on a Computer or Laptop*

🧭 *Step 1: Open Your Web Browser*

Use the internet browser you're comfortable with. Look for icons like:

- 🌐 Google Chrome
- 🧭 Safari
- ⚫ Microsoft Edge

Click to open it.

🔍 *Step 2: Go to Gmail*

In the address bar at the top of your screen, type:

```
CopyEdit
www.gmail.com
```

Then press **Enter.**

You'll land on the Gmail sign-in page.

21

Step 3: Enter Your Email Address

- You'll see a box that says **"Email or phone"**
- Type in the Gmail address you just created
  (Example: mary.johnson1954@gmail.com)

Click **Next**.

Step 4: Enter Your Password

- Type in the password you chose during sign-up
- Be careful with **capital letters** and **numbers**
- If your password is long or tricky, **use your notebook** to check it

Click **Next** again.

Step 5: Welcome to Your Gmail Inbox!

That's it! You'll see your inbox with a welcome message from Google and maybe a short tutorial. This is where all your new messages will appear.

Tip: Bookmark Gmail in your browser so you can come back easily:

- On most browsers, look for a ☆ (star) icon near the address bar
- Click it and save Gmail to your favorites

Option 2: Signing In on a Smartphone or Tablet

You might prefer using your phone or tablet—it's easy and convenient.

Step 1: Download the Gmail App

- **iPhone/iPad:** Open the App Store
- **Android:** Open the Google Play Store
- Search for "Gmail"
- Tap **Download** or **Install**

After it's installed, tap the **Gmail icon** to open it.

Step 2: Add Your Account

When you first open the app, it will ask:

"Add an email address?"

Tap **Google**, then tap **Continue** (if prompted).

Enter your **email address**, tap **Next**
Enter your **password**, tap **Next**

✅ That's it! You're in!

From now on, you can just tap the Gmail icon to check your messages anytime.

Common Questions and Helpful Tips

Q: What if I forget my password?
A: No problem. On the sign-in page, click **"Forgot password?"**
Gmail will guide you to reset it using your phone number or recovery email.

Q: Can I stay signed in?
A: Yes! On your personal computer or device, click **"Stay signed in"** or **check the box** so you don't have to enter your password every time.

Q: Is it safe to save my password?
A: If it's **your own device** and not shared, it's safe and convenient. Just don't save your password on public computers (like in a library).

✅ *Recap: What You Just Learned*

Step	What You Did
1	Opened your internet browser or Gmail app
2	Typed in your Gmail address
3	Entered your password carefully
4	Signed in successfully and saw your inbox

👏 You've now officially logged into Gmail—and the best part? You can do it again anytime you want, as often as you like.

Chapter 2: Exploring the Gmail Interface

🔧 The Inbox: Tabs and Sections Explained

(Understanding Your Gmail Inbox One Step at a Time)

Now that you've successfully signed in, you're probably looking at a page full of text and buttons. It might seem like a lot at first—but don't worry. You're not alone, and we'll break it down for you.

Think of your Gmail inbox like your **real-world mailbox**, but smarter. It doesn't just hold letters—it organizes them for you! Let's take a slow and easy tour of what you're looking at.

🖼️ *First Impression: What You See When You Log In*

Once you sign in, you're greeted by your **Inbox**. This is the main part of Gmail where all your emails arrive.

Right away, you'll notice:

- A **list of emails** in the middle of your screen
- Some **tabs at the top** of that list
- A **menu bar on the left** with more options (we'll talk more about that in the next section)

Let's focus on the inbox first.

📖 *The Inbox Tabs: What Are They?*

Gmail automatically **sorts your emails** into three sections called "tabs." These tabs help organize different types of messages so you can find things more easily.

Here's what each tab means:

1. **Primary (Main Inbox)**
   📌 This is where you'll find:
   - Messages from friends and family
   - Important updates from your bank, doctor, or subscriptions
   - Anything Gmail thinks you should see first
2. **Social**
   💬 This tab collects:
   - Notifications from Facebook, Instagram, Twitter, and other social media
   - You can ignore this if you don't use social media
3. **Promotions**
   🛍️ This one is for:
   - Ads and marketing emails (like discounts, sales, coupons)
   - It helps keep your main inbox uncluttered

💭 **Good to Know:**
If you want **everything in one place**, you can turn off the tabs later. But for now, it's helpful to let Gmail do the sorting.

📖 *The Email List: Reading Your Messages*

Each email in the list shows:

- The sender (who sent it)
- The subject (what the email is about)
- The first few words (a preview)
- The date or time it was sent

📌 **Unread emails** appear in **bold text** so they're easy to spot. Once you click on one, it opens in full.

To read an email:

1. Move your mouse or finger over the message you want
2. Click or tap it once
3. It will open in a new window or screen

To go back to your inbox:

- On a computer: Click the **back arrow** (usually top-left)
- On a phone: Tap the **back button** on your screen or use the navigation

Icons Next to Emails: What They Mean

You might notice small symbols or boxes beside each message:

- ✅ **Checkbox** – You can click it to select multiple emails
- ☆ **Star** – Mark important emails so you can find them later
- 📎 **Paperclip** – This email has an attachment (like a picture or document)

👉 Try clicking the **star icon** on a message from a friend—it highlights it for quick access later!

Gmail Is Smart!

Gmail is designed to **help you stay organized** without extra effort.

- Spam goes to the **Spam folder**
- Junk mail or newsletters are tucked into **Promotions**
- Real messages go into **Primary**

It's like having a little assistant sort your mail every day!

⚒ Quick Activity for Practice

Let's try it together:

1. Sign in to your Gmail
2. Look at the top tabs: **Primary**, **Social**, **Promotions**
3. Click on each one and explore what's inside
4. Open one email from **Primary**
5. Tap the ☆ star if you want to mark it as important
6. Click or tap "Back" to return to your inbox

👏 Great job! You're getting more familiar with Gmail already.

✅ Recap: What You've Learned

Feature	What It Does
Inbox	The main screen where your emails live
Tabs	Primary (important), Social, Promotions
Email List	Shows sender, subject, preview, date
Icons	Help you sort, star, and select emails

👴 Final Thought

Don't worry if it feels like a lot at once. The more you use Gmail, the more familiar it will become. And remember—you can always return to this guide for a refresher.

You're doing wonderfully. Be proud of yourself!

📁 Menu Bar and Icons

(Navigating Gmail's Menu and What All Those Icons Mean)

You've made it this far, and now it's time to dive into the **Menu Bar**—that strip of options on the left side of your screen. At first glance, it might seem like a jumble of icons and text, but don't worry! We're going to break it all down so you can use Gmail confidently.

Think of the **Menu Bar** as a **road map** to all the other parts of Gmail. Whether you need to send a message, look for old emails, or change settings, the menu bar is your guide.

🏠 *What's in the Menu Bar?*

The **Menu Bar** is located on the left side of your screen (or under the email list on your phone). It contains several options to navigate Gmail, and here's what they mean:

1. **Inbox** (🏠 Home Icon)
   - **Where your new messages live**. You've already seen this section, but this button lets you return here anytime. Clicking it takes you back to your inbox from any part of Gmail.
2. **Starred** (☆ Star Icon)
   - **Find emails you marked as important**. Whenever you tap that little **star** icon next to an email, it moves to this folder. It's a quick way to access your most important messages.
3. **Snoozed** (🕙 Clock Icon)
   - **Emails you've postponed** for later. If you're not ready to reply to a message yet but want to come back to it, you can snooze it to appear in your inbox later, on a day and time of your choosing.
4. **Sent** (🖃 Paper Plane Icon)
   - **Your outbox**. This folder contains all the emails you've sent to others. If you ever need to check something you've already sent, you can always find it here.
5. **Drafts** (✏ Pencil Icon)

- o **Emails you've started but haven't finished**. This folder saves your partially written emails. If you're interrupted while writing, you can come back later and pick up where you left off.
6. **Spam** (⊘ Trash Icon)
    - o **Unwanted or suspicious emails** that Gmail thinks are spam (junk mail). If Gmail mistakenly marks something as spam, you can move it back to your inbox.
7. **Trash** (🗑 Trash Can Icon)
    - o **Deleted messages**. If you accidentally delete an email, don't worry! It stays in the trash for about 30 days before being permanently deleted. You can restore it if needed.

⚒ *How to Use the Menu Bar Effectively*

The menu bar isn't just there to look pretty—it helps you manage your emails more easily. Here's how to use it effectively:

1. **Accessing Your Inbox Quickly:**
   When you're busy, the **Home (Inbox)** button is your best friend. Whenever you need to return to your main inbox, just click it, and you're back to where all your important messages are.
2. **Marking Important Emails:**
   If you get an email from a friend, family member, or someone you trust, you can mark it as **Starred**. This way, even if your inbox fills up, you'll always be able to find the important ones quickly.
3. **Handling Unwanted Emails:**
   Spam can be a nuisance, but Gmail is great at catching it for you. If you ever see an email in your inbox that you don't want, simply move it to **Spam** or **Trash** using the buttons at the top of the screen. This helps keep your inbox clean.
4. **Reviewing Sent Emails:**
   If you're waiting for a reply to an email you sent, you can easily check your **Sent** folder to see if you've received a response.

🐾 Understanding the Icons

Along with the main options in the menu bar, you'll notice a bunch of **icons** scattered around the Gmail interface. Here's what some of them mean:

1. **Search Bar** (🔍 Magnifying Glass Icon)
   - Want to find an email from someone? Or search for a specific word in an email? The search bar is your tool. Type anything, and Gmail will help you find it!
2. **Compose Button** (✏️ Pen Icon)
   - Ready to write a new email? Click the **Compose** button, and a new email window will pop up where you can add your recipient, subject, and message.
3. **Refresh Button** (🔄 Circular Arrow Icon)
   - Sometimes, your inbox doesn't update automatically. If you're waiting for a new email, hit the **refresh** button, and Gmail will check for new messages.
4. **Settings** (⚙️ Gear Icon)
   - This is where you can adjust your Gmail settings. Want to change your theme, manage your notifications, or update your password? The **gear icon** is where it all happens.

📱 Navigating the Menu Bar on Mobile

On your phone, the menu bar is a little different. Instead of a long list on the left, it's a **hamburger icon** (three stacked lines) in the top-left corner of the app. Tap this icon, and the menu will slide out, revealing the same options we've just discussed.

You can tap each section just like on the computer, and everything will update immediately.

🌥️ *Common Questions and Helpful Tips*

Q: How do I move emails from one folder to another?
A: It's easy! Just **select** the email (click or tap the checkbox), then look at the top for a **Move to** option. Choose where you want to move it (e.g., to **Spam**, **Trash**, or **Starred**).

Q: What if I want to customize my menu?
A: Gmail lets you **drag and drop** your folders in the menu bar! Click and hold any folder, then move it to a position you prefer.

Q: How can I stop spam emails from appearing in my inbox?
A: If you get a spam email, click the **Report Spam** button at the top of the email. Gmail will learn and improve its spam filter for next time.

✅ *Recap: What You've Learned*

Menu Section	What It Does
Inbox	Where your new emails are delivered
Starred	Stores important emails you've marked
Sent	Shows emails you've sent to others
Drafts	Stores incomplete emails that need finishing
Spam	Unwanted emails marked by Gmail as suspicious
Trash	Deleted emails (stay here for 30 days before disappearing)
Compose	Lets you write and send new emails
Search Bar	Helps you find emails quickly
Refresh	Updates your inbox with any new emails
Settings	Where you adjust your Gmail preferences

💡 *Final Thought*

Take a deep breath—you're doing great! The **Menu Bar** is a super useful tool, and now you know what each part of it does. The more you use it, the easier it will get. Every time you click on an icon or button, you're learning more about Gmail.

⚒ What Do All the Buttons Do? (Archive, Trash, Spam, etc.)

(Understanding Gmail's Buttons and How They Help You Manage Emails)

You've explored your inbox, learned about the menu bar, and now it's time to dive into the **buttons** that appear at the top of your Gmail screen. These buttons are there to help you **manage your emails**, and they might seem a bit overwhelming at first, but don't worry! We'll explain each one step by step, in simple terms.

Let's break down what each of these buttons does, and how they can help you stay organized and keep your Gmail running smoothly.

📥 Archive: Putting Emails Away Neatly

What is it?
The **Archive** button is like putting a letter into a **filing cabinet**—it's not trash, but you don't need it in your inbox anymore.

When you click **Archive**, the email is removed from your main inbox but **still accessible**. You can find it later by searching for it or by going to the **All Mail** section.

How do I use it?

- You've received an email, but it's something you don't need to read again soon, like a receipt or a notification.
- **Select the email** (by clicking the checkbox or tapping the email on your phone).
- Tap the **Archive** button (it looks like a **box with a down arrow**).

The email will disappear from your inbox, but you can still **search for it** later or look in **All Mail**.

Why use it?

- Keeps your inbox **clean** and free from clutter
- Allows you to **store** emails for future reference without them taking up space in your inbox

 Trash: Deleting Emails You Don't Need

What is it?

The **Trash** button is for when you want to **delete** emails that you no longer need, but don't want them to disappear right away. It's like throwing something into the trash bin, but it stays there for a while in case you change your mind.

When you hit the **Trash** button, the email will move to your **Trash folder**. It will remain there for **30 days**, after which it will be permanently deleted. But during those 30 days, you can **recover it** if you made a mistake.

How do I use it?

- Found an email you don't need, like a junk message or something you don't remember signing up for?
- **Select** the email (click the checkbox or tap the email).
- Tap the **Trash** button (it looks like a **trash can** icon).

Your email is now in **Trash**—it's still there if you need it, but it's no longer cluttering up your inbox.

Why use it?

- Helps you keep only the important emails in your inbox
- It's a simple way to get rid of emails you'll never need again
- It's like cleaning out your digital **junk drawer**!

⃠ *Spam: Flagging Unwanted or Suspicious Emails*

What is it?

The **Spam** button is used to tell Gmail that an email is **unwanted, unnecessary,** or **possibly dangerous**. Gmail's smart system will then move the email to your **Spam folder**, and it'll no longer show up in your inbox. It's like telling a friend, "Don't send me this again!"

But, be careful: Sometimes, important emails might end up in Spam by mistake.

How do I use it?

- If you get an email from an unknown sender or something that looks **suspicious**, it's probably spam.
- **Select** the email (click the checkbox or tap the email).
- Tap the **Spam** button (it looks like a **stop sign** or **triangle with an exclamation point**).

Now the email will go into your **Spam folder** and Gmail will remember not to show you similar messages in the future.

Why use it?

- Helps you avoid **unwanted junk mail**
- Keeps your inbox free of **spammy** or possibly harmful emails
- It's like keeping your mailbox safe from **strange** or **unwanted** letters

☆ *Star: Marking Important Emails*

What is it?

The **Star** button lets you mark an email as **important**. It's like putting a sticky note on something you want to remember or follow up on later. Starred emails are easy to find, even if they're buried in a sea of other messages.

How do I use it?

- If you get an email from a friend, family member, or someone you need to remember to respond to later, just **click the star** next to the email.
- Once the email is starred, you can find it anytime by going to your **Starred folder**.

Why use it?

- Keeps important messages **easily accessible**
- Helps you find emails you need to **follow up on**
- It's a quick and easy way to **organize** emails without deleting or archiving them

 *Refresh: Checking for New Emails*

What is it?

Sometimes, your inbox doesn't update right away. If you're waiting for a new message, tap the **Refresh** button to force Gmail to check for new emails.

How do I use it?

- Tap the **Refresh button** (usually represented by a **circular arrow**).
- It will refresh your inbox and show you any new messages that have come in.

Why use it?

- Ensures you're **not missing anything** important
- Quick way to **update** your inbox manually when you think new emails should have arrived

⚙️ *Settings: Customizing Your Gmail*

What is it?

The **Settings** button is where you can adjust how Gmail looks and behaves. This includes changing your email theme, adjusting notifications, or setting up security options. You can make Gmail more personal and **comfortable** to use by adjusting these settings.

How do I use it?

- Click or tap on the **gear icon** at the top-right of Gmail.
- A drop-down menu will appear, where you can choose **Settings** to make changes to things like **display**, **notifications**, and even **language**.

Why use it?

- You can **personalize** your Gmail experience to fit your preferences
- Adjust settings to help you manage how emails are displayed or organized
- It's like arranging your desk to be **just the way you like it**!

✅ *Recap: The Buttons You've Learned About*

Button	What It Does
Archive	Puts emails away without deleting them
Trash	Deletes emails (keeps them for 30 days)
Spam	Flags unwanted or suspicious emails
Star	Marks important emails for easy reference
Refresh	Manually checks for new emails
Settings	Lets you customize Gmail's appearance and settings

💡 *Final Thought*

There you have it! You now know what each of these **buttons** does and how to use them to keep your Gmail clean, organized, and working for you. Don't worry if you need to look back at this section every now and then—practice makes perfect, and you'll feel more comfortable as you go along.

⚒ What Do All the Buttons Do? (Archive, Trash, Spam, etc.)

(Understanding Gmail's Buttons and How They Help You Manage Emails)

You've explored your inbox, learned about the menu bar, and now it's time to dive into the **buttons** that appear at the top of your Gmail screen. These buttons are there to help you **manage your emails**, and they might seem a bit overwhelming at first, but don't worry! We'll explain each one step by step, in simple terms.

Let's break down what each of these buttons does, and how they can help you stay organized and keep your Gmail running smoothly.

🗄 *Archive: Putting Emails Away Neatly*

What is it?
The **Archive** button is like putting a letter into a **filing cabinet**—it's not trash, but you don't need it in your inbox anymore.

When you click **Archive**, the email is removed from your main inbox but **still accessible**. You can find it later by searching for it or by going to the **All Mail** section.

How do I use it?

- You've received an email, but it's something you don't need to read again soon, like a receipt or a notification.
- **Select the email** (by clicking the checkbox or tapping the email on your phone).
- Tap the **Archive** button (it looks like a **box with a down arrow**).

The email will disappear from your inbox, but you can still **search for it** later or look in **All Mail**.

Why use it?

- Keeps your inbox **clean** and free from clutter
- Allows you to **store** emails for future reference without them taking up space in your inbox

 Trash: Deleting Emails You Don't Need

What is it?

The **Trash** button is for when you want to **delete** emails that you no longer need, but don't want them to disappear right away. It's like throwing something into the trash bin, but it stays there for a while in case you change your mind.

When you hit the **Trash** button, the email will move to your **Trash folder**. It will remain there for **30 days**, after which it will be permanently deleted. But during those 30 days, you can **recover it** if you made a mistake.

How do I use it?

- Found an email you don't need, like a junk message or something you don't remember signing up for?
- **Select** the email (click the checkbox or tap the email).
- Tap the **Trash** button (it looks like a **trash can** icon).

Your email is now in **Trash**—it's still there if you need it, but it's no longer cluttering up your inbox.

Why use it?

- Helps you keep only the important emails in your inbox
- It's a simple way to get rid of emails you'll never need again
- It's like cleaning out your digital **junk drawer**!

⊘ Spam: Flagging Unwanted or Suspicious Emails

What is it?

The **Spam** button is used to tell Gmail that an email is **unwanted**, **unnecessary**, or **possibly dangerous**. Gmail's smart system will then move the email to your **Spam folder**, and it'll no longer show up in your inbox. It's like telling a friend, "Don't send me this again!"

But, be careful: Sometimes, important emails might end up in Spam by mistake.

How do I use it?

- If you get an email from an unknown sender or something that looks **suspicious**, it's probably spam.
- **Select** the email (click the checkbox or tap the email).
- Tap the **Spam** button (it looks like a **stop sign** or **triangle with an exclamation point**).

Now the email will go into your **Spam folder** and Gmail will remember not to show you similar messages in the future.

Why use it?

- Helps you avoid **unwanted junk mail**
- Keeps your inbox free of **spammy** or possibly harmful emails
- It's like keeping your mailbox safe from **strange** or **unwanted** letters

☆ Star: Marking Important Emails

What is it?

The **Star** button lets you mark an email as **important**. It's like putting a sticky note on something you want to remember or follow up on later. Starred emails are easy to find, even if they're buried in a sea of other messages.

How do I use it?

- If you get an email from a friend, family member, or someone you need to remember to respond to later, just **click the star** next to the email.
- Once the email is starred, you can find it anytime by going to your **Starred folder**.

Why use it?

- Keeps important messages **easily accessible**
- Helps you find emails you need to **follow up on**
- It's a quick and easy way to **organize** emails without deleting or archiving them

🔄 Refresh: Checking for New Emails

What is it?

Sometimes, your inbox doesn't update right away. If you're waiting for a new message, tap the **Refresh** button to force Gmail to check for new emails.

How do I use it?

- Tap the **Refresh button** (usually represented by a **circular arrow**).
- It will refresh your inbox and show you any new messages that have come in.

Why use it?

- Ensures you're **not missing anything** important
- Quick way to **update** your inbox manually when you think new emails should have arrived

⚙ *Settings: Customizing Your Gmail*

What is it?

The **Settings** button is where you can adjust how Gmail looks and behaves. This includes changing your email theme, adjusting notifications, or setting up security options. You can make Gmail more personal and **comfortable** to use by adjusting these settings.

How do I use it?

- Click or tap on the **gear icon** at the top-right of Gmail.
- A drop-down menu will appear, where you can choose **Settings** to make changes to things like **display**, **notifications**, and even **language**.

Why use it?

- You can **personalize** your Gmail experience to fit your preferences
- Adjust settings to help you manage how emails are displayed or organized
- It's like arranging your desk to be **just the way you like it**!

✔️ *Recap: The Buttons You've Learned About*

Button	What It Does
Archive	Puts emails away without deleting them
Trash	Deletes emails (keeps them for 30 days)
Spam	Flags unwanted or suspicious emails
Star	Marks important emails for easy reference
Refresh	Manually checks for new emails
Settings	Lets you customize Gmail's appearance and settings

💡 *Final Thought*

There you have it! You now know what each of these **buttons** does and how to use them to keep your Gmail clean, organized, and working for you. Don't worry if you need to look back at this section every now and then—practice makes perfect, and you'll feel more comfortable as you go along.

Chapter 3: Sending and Receiving Emails

🗳 How to Compose a New Email

(Starting a Conversation, the Easy Way)

So, you've logged into Gmail, and now you're ready to write your very first email. Congratulations! 🎉 Email is a fantastic way to stay connected with your family, friends, doctors, service providers—even your favorite stores and newsletters.

This section will walk you through everything you need to know about composing a new email—**in simple steps, without any rush or tech jargon.**

✉ *What Does "Compose" Mean?*

Think of "compose" like sitting down to write a letter—but instead of pen and paper, you're using your keyboard. When you "compose" an email, you're writing a message that you will send to someone's inbox, and they'll be able to read it almost instantly.

🖰 *Step-By-Step: Composing an Email on Your Computer*

Let's get started! Follow these easy steps to write a new email from your computer:

1. **Open Gmail in your browser** (like Chrome or Safari).
2. Look at the top-left of your Gmail screen.
3. You'll see a big **"+ Compose"** button. It's usually red or white with a plus sign.
   👉 **Click on that.**

4. A small email window will pop up—this is your blank canvas!
5. Here's what you'll see and what goes where:

📄 What Goes Where in a New Email?

Section	What You Type Here
To:	The email address of the person you're sending it to. Example: `granddaughter123@gmail.com`
Subject:	A short title that tells the person what the email is about. Example: "Birthday Photos" or "Update on My Doctor Visit"
Main Box:	This is your message space! You can write just like you would in a letter—start with a greeting, add your thoughts, and end with your name.

✏️ Example Email

Here's what a simple message might look like:

- **To:** `john.smith@example.com`
- **Subject:** *Lunch This Sunday?*
- **Message:**

```
vbnet
CopyEdit
Hi John,

Just wondering if you're free for lunch this Sunday. It's been a while,
and I'd love to catch up!
```

```
Let me know what works for you.

Warmly,
Mary
```

💡 *Don't worry about grammar or spelling too much. Just write from the heart, and people will understand!*

📧 *How to Send the Email*

Once you're done writing your message, sending it is the easy part:

- Click the **blue "Send" button** at the bottom left of the message window.
- Poof! Your email has flown off to its destination—just like magic.

🎉 That's it! You've just composed and sent an email.

📱 *How to Compose an Email on a Phone or Tablet*

Don't worry—composing an email on a mobile device is just as easy:

1. Open the **Gmail app**.
2. Tap the red **"Compose"** button (usually at the bottom right).
3. You'll see fields for **To**, **Subject**, and your message—just like on the computer.
4. When you're done, tap the **paper plane icon** (send button) at the top.

💡 *Tip:* You can even talk into your phone and have it type your message. Look for the microphone icon on your keyboard!

😊 *Common Questions from Seniors*

Q: What if I make a mistake?

A: No problem! You can hit **Backspace** to erase, or even click "Discard" (trash icon) if you want to start fresh.

Q: Can I save a message to finish later?

A: Absolutely! Gmail automatically saves your email as a **draft**. You can find it in the left-hand menu under "Drafts" and continue anytime.

Q: Can I send to more than one person?

A: Yes! You can add multiple email addresses in the **"To"** field, separated by commas. We'll talk more about group emails later in this chapter.

🕐 *Quick Recap*

- ✔ Click "Compose"
- ✔ Fill in the **To**, **Subject**, and **Message**
- ✔ Click **Send**
- ✔ That's it—you've sent your message!

💬 *Final Encouragement*

Think of each email as a little piece of yourself you're sending out into the world. It might be a warm greeting, a question, a thank-you, or even a funny story. The beauty of email is that it helps you **stay connected—anytime, anywhere.**

You don't need to be a tech expert. Just one click at a time, and you'll be amazed how natural it starts to feel.

📎 Adding an Attachment (Photo or File)

(How to Share Special Moments and Important Documents by Email)

Have you ever wanted to send a photo of your grandkids, a recipe, or a scanned document—like a medical form or an invitation—to someone by email? Well, with Gmail, it's not just possible—it's easy!

In this section, we'll walk through exactly how to attach a photo or a file to your email. Just think of it like slipping a picture or paper into an envelope before mailing it. Let's take it slow, and you'll be doing it like a pro in no time!

📁 What Is an Attachment?

An *attachment* is any file you add to your email—like a:

- 📷 Photo or image
- 📄 PDF document
- 📝 Word or text file
- 📊 Spreadsheet

If it's stored on your computer or phone, chances are you can send it through Gmail.

💻 How to Attach a File on a Computer (Step-by-Step)

Let's begin with how to add a file using a laptop or desktop:

1. **Open Gmail** and click **"Compose"** to start a new email.
2. Fill in the **To**, **Subject**, and your message—just like we covered in the last section.
3. Now look at the bottom of the email window. You'll see several little icons. Hover your mouse over them. One looks like a **paperclip**.
   🔍 **That's the Attach File button!**

4. Click the **paperclip icon** 📎. A window will pop up showing files and folders from your computer.
5. Find the file you want to send:
   ○ For photos, look in the **Pictures** folder.
   ○ For documents, try **Documents** or your **Desktop**.
6. Click the file, then click **Open**.

✅ That's it! You'll see the file added to the bottom of your email message. It's now "attached."

7. Click **Send** like usual, and your message—with the file—is on its way!

🖼️ *Example: Sending a Photo to a Grandchild*

Let's say you want to send a picture from your birthday party.

- **Click Compose**
- **Add a message:** "Hi sweetheart, here's a photo from last weekend. Love you!"
- **Click the paperclip icon**
- **Choose the photo file from your Pictures folder**
- **Click Open**
- **Send it!** 📩

📌 *The person you send it to will receive both your message and the photo together.*

📱 *How to Attach a File on a Phone or Tablet*

Want to send a photo straight from your phone? Here's how:

1. Open the **Gmail app** and tap the **"Compose"** button.
2. Fill in your email like usual.
3. Tap the **paperclip icon** or sometimes a **paperclip + "Attach file"** option in the menu.
4. Choose whether to attach:

- A photo from your gallery
- A file from your phone storage

5. Tap the file you want, and it will appear in your message.

Tip: On Android phones, you might need to choose "Attach file" or "Insert from Drive." On iPhones, you may be asked to allow Gmail access to your photos. Just tap **Allow**.

FAQs and Gentle Reminders

Q: Is there a limit to file size?
A: Yes—Gmail lets you send files up to **25MB**. If it's larger (like a video), Gmail will offer to send it using **Google Drive** instead. Don't worry—we'll explain that later in the book.

Q: Can I attach more than one file?
A: Absolutely! Just repeat the steps above and select more files. Gmail lets you attach multiple items to one email.

Q: What if I change my mind?
A: No problem! Hover over the attachment and click the **"X"** to remove it before you hit send.

Pro Tips

- **Organize your files.** It's easier to find them when they're in a folder you recognize (like "Photos" or "My Documents").
- **Scanning paper documents?** Use a scanner or an app like "Google Drive" or "Notes" to turn papers into digital files you can attach.
- **Mention your attachment** in the message:
  "Please find the doctor's note attached."

---

1. Start a new email.
2. Click or tap the **paperclip** icon.
3. Choose the file or photo.
4. Attach it.
5. Send it with a smile! 😊

🏠 *Final Encouragement*

Learning to add attachments can open a world of communication! You'll be able to share **precious memories**, **important papers**, and **special moments** with just a few clicks. And the more you practice, the more natural it will feel.

Take your time—and don't be afraid to try. The "Undo" button is your friend, and nothing is too hard when we break it down together.

📬 Replying and Forwarding Emails

(Keeping Conversations Going & Sharing Messages with Others)

Emails aren't just about sending messages—you'll also receive them. And just like with letters in the mail, you might want to write back **or** pass the message along **to someone else. This section will show you how to reply and forward emails like a pro—step by step, with clarity and confidence.**

Let's break it all down together. You'll be amazed at how natural it becomes!

🔲 *What Does "Reply" Mean?*

When someone sends you an email, and you want to respond directly to them, that's called a **Reply**. It's like writing a letter back to a friend who just wrote to you.

✔ When you click **Reply**, Gmail opens a window where you can type your message. Your reply will go back to the **same person** who sent the original email.

Example:
Your daughter sends you a photo and says, "Hope you're feeling better!"
You click **Reply** and type: "Thank you, sweetheart! I'm doing much better."

🔄 *What Does "Forward" Mean?*

Forwarding an email means you're sending the message **you received** to **someone else**. Imagine you got a helpful article from a friend and you think another friend might enjoy it too—you forward it to them.

✔ When you click **Forward**, you choose a new person to send the email to, and you can add your own note on top of the original message.

Example:
You receive a recipe for apple pie from a friend. You click **Forward** and send it to your sister, writing: "You'll love this!"

💻 *How to Reply to an Email on a Computer (Step-by-Step)*

Let's go through replying first:

1. Open **Gmail** on your computer.
2. Click on the **email you received** (it will be in your Inbox).
3. Scroll down to the bottom of the message.
4. You'll see two options: **Reply** or **Forward**.
   Click **Reply**.

📝 A new message box will appear under the original message.

5. Type your reply in the box.
6. Click the **blue "Send"** button when you're done.

🎉 Congratulations! You've replied to an email!

📤 *How to Forward an Email (Step-by-Step)*

Now let's forward that same message:

1. Open the email you want to share.
2. Click **Forward** (next to the Reply button).
3. A new box opens—this time, type the **email address** of the person you're sending it to.
4. You can also type a short message above the original email, like:
   "Hi Tom, thought this might interest you!"
5. Click **Send** when ready.

Tip: The person you forward the email to will also see the original message unless you delete it from the body.

Replying and Forwarding on a Phone or Tablet

Using a smartphone? No worries—we've got you:

To Reply:

1. Tap the Gmail app and open the email.
2. Tap the **arrow icon** (or sometimes just says **Reply**) near the bottom.
3. Type your response.
4. Tap the **Send** icon (paper airplane at the top).

To Forward:

1. Open the email.
2. Tap the **three dots** (⋮ or …) in the upper-right or lower corner.
3. Choose **Forward**.
4. Enter the recipient's email address.
5. Tap **Send**.

Don't worry if you tap the wrong option—you can always go back and try again!

Common Questions from Seniors

Q: Will the person see the original message when I forward?
Yes. Everything in the original email will be included, unless you manually delete it.

Q: Can I reply to everyone if there were multiple senders?
Yes! Click **Reply All** to respond to everyone at once. This is helpful for family group emails or event planning.

Q: What if I forget to reply?

⬤ Gmail often reminds you with a gentle note like "You received this 3 days ago—want to reply?"

📁 *Helpful Terms to Remember*

- **Reply:** Sends your message back to the sender only.
- **Reply All:** Sends your message to everyone the email was sent to.
- **Forward:** Sends the email to someone new, outside the original group.

🕐 *Recap Time*

Action	Use It When…	Result
Reply	You want to answer someone directly	Sends your message to 1 person
Reply All	You're replying to a group conversation	Sends your reply to all recipients
Forward	You want to share an email with someone new	They get the original message too

---

⊚ *Practice Tip*

Try this exercise:

1. Ask a friend or family member to send you a test email.
2. Open it.
3. Click **Reply** and write back a simple message.
4. Then open another email and **Forward** it to someone else.

⬤ Practice builds confidence—and you're doing amazing!

Final Encouragement

Emails are conversations—and now you know how to keep them going! Whether you're replying with thanks, forwarding fun photos, or sharing a laugh, you're mastering the digital version of pen-pal magic.

Don't rush it. The more you reply and forward, the easier it will feel. You're becoming a Gmail whiz, one click at a time!

⬆ Using CC and BCC

(Who Else Should See Your Email… and Who Shouldn't?)

When sending an email, sometimes you want more than one person to read it, **and other times, you want to** keep someone in the loop privately. **That's where** CC **and** BCC **come in—two little options with big powers.**

Don't worry if these sound confusing! We're going to walk through them step-by-step, with simple real-life examples, so you'll know exactly when and how to use them.

😀 What Do "CC" and "BCC" Mean?

Let's break it down:

- **CC** stands for **Carbon Copy**.
- **BCC** stands for **Blind Carbon Copy**.

Yes, the terms come from the days of typewriters and carbon paper—but don't let that throw you off. In email terms, it's all about **sending a copy** of the message.

⚪ What is CC (Carbon Copy)?

When you **CC** someone, it means you're **sending them a copy of the email**, but you're not writing it directly to them. Everyone who receives the email can see that the person was CC'd.

📌 *It's like including someone in a group letter, just so they know what's going on— even if you're not talking directly to them.*

Example:
You send an email to your plumber, and you **CC your daughter** so she knows the plumber is coming over.

💭 Think of it like saying: "Hey, I'm not talking to you directly, but I thought you'd like to know about this."

🌑 What is BCC (Blind Carbon Copy)?

When you **BCC** someone, you're also sending them a copy of the email—but here's the difference:
No one else will know they got it. Their email is **hidden** from everyone else.

📌 *It's like sending a secret copy of a letter to someone, without the main recipient knowing.*

Example:
You email your friend about a surprise birthday party and **BCC your other friend**, so they know the plan—but the first person doesn't see that you included them.

💭 Think of BCC as your "discreet mode."

💻 How to Use CC and BCC on a Computer

Let's say you're writing a new email. Here's how to add CC and BCC fields:

1. Open Gmail and click **"Compose"** (the big button on the left).
2. A new message window opens.
   You'll see a line that says **To:** — this is where you type the main person's email address.
3. On the right side of that line, click **"CC"** or **"BCC"** — they'll appear just under the "To" field.

📝 Now you can type other email addresses into those new boxes!

- Use the **CC field** for people you want to include publicly.
- Use the **BCC field** for people you want to include privately.

4. Add your message, then click **Send**—and Gmail does the rest!

📱 *How to Use CC and BCC on a Phone or Tablet*

If you're using the Gmail app:

1. Tap **Compose** to write a new email.
2. Tap the small **arrow down** next to the **To** field (this reveals CC/BCC).
3. Now you'll see the **CC** and **BCC** fields appear.
4. Add addresses as needed, type your message, and hit **Send**.

📌 It's just a matter of tapping that arrow!

🤓 *Real-Life Scenarios for CC and BCC*

Let's make this even more practical. Here are a few examples of when to use each:

✔️ *Good Times to Use CC:*

- You're sending a photo to your niece and want your daughter to see it too.
- You're confirming an appointment with your doctor and want your spouse in the loop.

✔️ *Good Times to Use BCC:*

- You're inviting your entire book club but want to **keep their emails private**.
- You're forwarding an article to several friends without letting them know who else got it.

📌 *BCC is great for privacy, CC is great for openness.*

☁ *Common Questions from Seniors*

Q: Will the person in BCC know they were BCC'd?

⚪ Yes, **they** will see the email—but **others will not** know they were included.

Q: Can I use both CC and BCC at the same time?

⚪ Absolutely. Gmail allows you to mix and match based on who should see what.

Q: Is it rude to BCC someone?

⚪ Not at all—it's actually polite in many cases. It protects other people's privacy, especially when sending group messages.

💬 *Let's Practice Together!*

Try this activity:

1. Compose a new email to a family member.
2. Add another relative in the **CC** field.
3. Add a close friend in the **BCC** field (just for fun and practice).
4. Type a message like:
   "Hey, just testing out CC and BCC in Gmail. Hope this works!"
5. Click **Send**.

🎉 Boom! You've now mastered the mystery of CC and BCC.

☺ *Final Encouragement*

The more you use email, the more confident you'll become. With CC and BCC in your toolbelt, you're not just using Gmail—you're using it **smartly**.

Never be afraid to experiment. Try sending a few test messages to yourself or a family member to see how things show up. You're doing amazing, and each chapter brings you one step closer to tech mastery!

📬 Still with us?
We hope you're enjoying your journey with Gmail! 😊
If you've found the guide useful so far, a kind review would mean a lot. Just a few words on Amazon can help more people discover this helpful resource. Thank you! ♡

📢 Sending Group Emails

(Effortlessly Communicate with Multiple People at Once)

Imagine you want to send the same email to your book club members, family, **or** volunteer group. **Instead of typing each email address individually, Gmail allows you to create a** group—**making it simple to send messages to multiple people simultaneously.**

In this section, we'll explore how to create, manage, **and** send emails to groups **in Gmail, ensuring you stay connected with your communities effortlessly.**

😊 What Is a Group Email?

A **group email** in Gmail is a feature that lets you **bundle multiple contacts under a single label**. Once created, you can use this label to send an email to all members of the group without entering each address manually.

Example:
You create a group labeled **"Family"**. When composing an email, you simply type "Family" in the recipient field, and Gmail sends the message to everyone in that group.

💻 Creating a Group Email Using Google Contacts

To set up a group email, we'll use **Google Contacts**, which integrates seamlessly with Gmail.

Step-by-Step Guide:

1. **Access Google Contacts:**
   - Open your web browser and go to Google Contacts.
   - Ensure you're logged in with your Gmail account.
2. **Select Contacts for the Group:**

- o Browse through your list and **check the boxes** next to the contacts you want to include in the group.
3. **Create a New Label:**
   - o After selecting contacts, click the **label icon** (it looks like a tag) at the top of the page.
   - o Choose **"Create label"** from the dropdown menu.
4. **Name Your Label:**
   - o Enter a descriptive name for your group, such as **"Book Club"** or **"Family"**.
   - o Click **"Save"** to create the label.
5. **Verify the Group:**
   - o On the left sidebar under **"Labels"**, click your newly created label to see all contacts associated with it.

📧 Sending an Email to Your Group

Now that your group is set up, sending an email is straightforward.

Step-by-Step Guide:

1. **Compose a New Email:**
   - o Open Gmail and click the **"Compose"** button.
2. **Enter the Group Name:**
   - o In the **"To"** field, type the name of your label (e.g., "Book Club").
   - o Gmail will auto-suggest the label; select it.
3. **Draft Your Message:**
   - o Enter your **subject** and **email content** as you normally would.
4. **Send the Email:**
   - o Click **"Send"**, and your message will be delivered to all group members.

📱 Managing Group Emails on Mobile Devices

While creating labels is best done on a computer, you can still send group emails from your mobile device.

To Send a Group Email on Mobile:

1. **Open the Gmail App:**
   - Tap the **"Compose"** button.
2. **Enter the Group Name:**
   - In the **"To"** field, type the label name you've created.
   - Select it when it appears.
3. **Compose and Send:**
   - Write your email and tap **"Send"**.

Note: To create or manage labels on mobile, consider using the Google Contacts app for Android or access Google Contacts via a web browser on iOS devices.

⚒ *Editing or Deleting a Group*

To Add or Remove Contacts from a Group:

1. **Access Google Contacts:**
   - Navigate to Google Contacts.
2. **Select the Contact:**
   - Check the box next to the contact you wish to modify.
3. **Manage Labels:**
   - Click the **label icon** and check or uncheck the relevant labels.
   - Click **"Apply"** to save changes.

To Delete a Group:

1. **In Google Contacts:**
   - On the left sidebar under **"Labels"**, hover over the label you want to delete.
2. **Delete the Label:**
   - Click the **trash can icon** that appears.
   - Confirm the deletion.

Note: Deleting a label does **not** remove the contacts; it only deletes the group label.

Common Questions

Q: Can I send an email without recipients seeing each other's addresses?
A: Yes, use the **BCC (Blind Carbon Copy)** field. Enter your own email in the **"To"** field and the group label in the **"BCC"** field. This way, recipients won't see each other's email addresses.

Q: Is there a limit to how many contacts I can add to a group?
A: Gmail allows you to add a substantial number of contacts to a group. However, be mindful of Gmail's sending limits to avoid your account being flagged for spam.

Q: Can I create multiple groups?
A: Absolutely! You can create as many groups (labels) as needed to organize your contacts effectively.

Practice Activity

1. **Create a Group:**
   o Follow the steps above to create a group labeled **"Friends"**.
2. **Send a Test Email:**
   o Compose an email to your new group with a friendly message.
3. **Verify Delivery:**
   o Check with a few recipients to ensure they received the email.

By practicing, you'll become more comfortable with managing group emails.

☺ Final Encouragement

Mastering group emails in Gmail enhances your communication efficiency, allowing you to stay connected with various circles effortlessly. Remember, technology is a tool to serve you—take your time, practice, and soon it will feel second nature.

You're doing wonderfully on this journey. Keep exploring, and don't hesitate to revisit sections as needed. Each step forward is a step toward greater digital confidence.

Chapter 4: Staying Organized

📁 Labels vs. Folders: What's the Difference?

(Understanding the Tools to Organize Your Inbox Effectively)

In the realm of email management, organizing your messages is crucial for efficiency and ease of access. Two primary tools facilitate this organization: folders and labels. While they may seem similar, they serve distinct functions and offer different advantages. Let's explore these tools in depth to enhance your email organization skills.

😊 *What Are Folders?*

Folders are a traditional method of organizing emails, akin to physical file folders. They allow you to store emails in separate compartments based on categories or topics.

Key Characteristics of Folders:

- **Exclusive Containment:** An email can reside in only one folder at a time. Placing an email into a folder moves it from the inbox to that specific folder.
- **Hierarchical Structure:** Folders often support subfolders, enabling a tree-like organization. For example:
    - **Family**
        - Parents
        - Siblings
    - **Work**
        - Projects
            - Project A
            - Project B

Analogy: Think of folders as drawers in a filing cabinet, where each drawer holds documents pertaining to a specific subject.

☐ What Are Labels?

Labels offer a more dynamic approach to email organization, particularly popularized by platforms like Gmail.

Key Characteristics of Labels:

- **Multiple Assignments:** Unlike folders, you can assign multiple labels to a single email. This means an email can simultaneously belong to several categories.
- **Non-Movement:** Applying a label doesn't move the email from the inbox; it simply tags it for easy retrieval.
- **Color-Coding:** Many email services allow color-coding labels for visual distinction.

Analogy: Imagine labels as sticky notes attached to documents, where a single document can have multiple sticky notes indicating different categories or priorities.

🔑 Key Differences Between Folders and Labels

Aspect	Folders	Labels
Uniqueness	An email resides in one folder at a time.	An email can have multiple labels simultaneously.
Movement	Moving an email to a folder removes it from the inbox.	Labeling an email doesn't remove it from the inbox.
Structure	Supports hierarchical organization with subfolders.	Generally flat structure, though some services allow nested labels.
Flexibility	Less flexible due to exclusive containment.	More flexible, allowing cross-categorization of emails.

🔲 *Practical Implications*

When to Use Folders:

- **Exclusive Categorization:** When emails fit neatly into a single category without overlap.
- **Structured Organization:** If you prefer a clear, hierarchical structure for your emails.

When to Use Labels:

- **Multiple Contexts:** When emails pertain to multiple categories or projects.
- **Enhanced Searchability:** Labels facilitate finding emails through various categorical tags.

Combining Both:

Some email platforms allow the use of both folders and labels, enabling you to tailor your organization system to your preferences. For instance, you might use folders for broad categories and labels for specific tags or priorities.

😐 *Considerations for Seniors*

Understanding the nuances between folders and labels can significantly enhance your email management experience. Here are some tailored tips:

- **Start Simple:** Begin by creating a few broad folders or labels that reflect your primary email categories (e.g., Family, Health, Finances).
- **Experiment:** Don't hesitate to experiment with both systems to find what aligns best with your workflow.
- **Seek Assistance:** If unsure, consult with family members or tech-savvy friends to set up an organization system that suits your needs.

💬 *Interactive Exercise*

Objective: Create a folder and a label in your email account to experience the difference firsthand.

Steps:

1. **Creating a Folder:**
    - Navigate to your email platform's folder management section.
    - Select the option to create a new folder.
    - Name the folder (e.g., "Family").
    - Move a relevant email into this folder.
2. **Creating a Label:**
    - Navigate to your email platform's label management section.
    - Select the option to create a new label.
    - Name the label (e.g., "Health").
    - Apply this label to a relevant email without moving it from the inbox.

Reflection: Observe how the email behaves in each scenario. Note the differences in accessibility and organization.

😊 *Final Thoughts*

Mastering the use of folders and labels can transform your email experience, making communication more organized and less overwhelming. By understanding and utilizing these tools, you can tailor your inbox to reflect your personal preferences and needs.

Remember, the goal is to create a system that feels intuitive and enhances your digital correspondence. Don't be afraid to adjust and refine your approach as you become more comfortable with these tools.

📁 Creating Folders for Friends, Family, Doctors, etc.

(Organize Your Inbox by Categorizing Emails into Specific Folders)

Effectively managing your email correspondence is essential for maintaining a clutter-free inbox and ensuring important messages are easily accessible. By creating specific folders (known as labels **in Gmail) for different categories—such as** Friends, Family, Doctors, **and more—you can streamline your email organization. This section will guide you through the process of setting up these folders and utilizing them efficiently.**

😊 *Understanding Labels in Gmail*

In Gmail, **labels** function similarly to traditional folders but offer enhanced flexibility:

- **Multiple Labels:** An email can have multiple labels, allowing it to exist in several categories simultaneously.
- **Color-Coding:** Labels can be color-coded for visual distinction, making it easier to identify emails at a glance.
- **Nested Labels:** You can create sub-labels under a main label to further organize your emails hierarchically.Email Genie

---

💻 *Creating Labels for Specific Categories*

Step-by-Step Guide:

1. **Access Gmail:**
   - Open your web browser and navigate to Gmail.
   - Ensure you're logged into your account.
2. **Initiate Label Creation:**

- On the left sidebar, scroll down and click on **"More"** to expand additional options.Google Help+2Sales Engagement Made Easy | Yesware+2Google Help+2
- Click on **"Create new label"**.Email Genie+2Google Help+2Google Help+2

3. **Name Your Label:**
   - In the pop-up window, enter a descriptive name for your label, such as **"Friends"**, **"Family"**, or **"Doctors"**.
   - Click **"Create"** to finalize.

4. **Assign a Color (Optional):**
   - Locate your newly created label on the left sidebar.
   - Hover over it and click the **three vertical dots** (more options).Sales Engagement Made Easy | Yesware+1Email Genie+1
   - Select **"Label color"** and choose a color to associate with this label.Email Genie

---

📧 Applying Labels to Emails

Once your labels are set up, you can start organizing your emails:

1. **Labeling Existing Emails:**
   - Open an email you wish to categorize.
   - Click on the **label icon** (it resembles a tag) at the top of the email.
   - Check the box next to the appropriate label(s) and click **"Apply"**.

2. **Labeling Incoming Emails Automatically:**
   - In Gmail, click on the **search bar** at the top and then the **filter icon** (it looks like three horizontal lines).
   - Set criteria for the filter (e.g., emails from a specific sender).
   - Click **"Create filter"**.
   - Check **"Apply the label"** and choose the relevant label.Time
   - Click **"Create filter"** to finalize.

📱 *Managing Labels on Mobile Devices*

You can also create and manage labels using the Gmail mobile app:

1. **Open the Gmail App:**
   - Launch the Gmail app on your smartphone or tablet.Sales Engagement Made Easy | Yesware
2. **Access Label Management:**
   - Tap the **menu icon** (three horizontal lines) in the top-left corner.Sales Engagement Made Easy | Yesware+1activeinboxhq.com+1
   - Scroll down and tap **"Create new"** under the **Labels** section.Sales Engagement Made Easy | Yesware+2activeinboxhq.com+2Email Genie+2
3. **Name and Save the Label:**
   - Enter a name for your label (e.g., "Doctors").
   - Tap **"Done"** or **"Save"** to create the label.

🛠️ *Editing or Deleting Labels*

To Edit a Label:

1. In Gmail, find the label on the left sidebar.
2. Hover over it and click the **three vertical dots**.
3. Select **"Edit"**, make your changes, and click **"Save"**.

To Delete a Label:

1. Hover over the label and click the **three vertical dots**.Sales Engagement Made Easy | Yesware+1Email Genie+1
2. Select **"Remove label"**.Reddit+3Sales Engagement Made Easy | Yesware+3Email Genie+3
3. Confirm the deletion when prompted.

Note: Deleting a label does not delete the emails associated with it; it only removes the label from those emails.

😶 Common Questions

Q: Can I nest labels under a main category?
A: Yes, Gmail allows you to create sub-labels (nested labels) under a main label. When creating or editing a label, check the box for **"Nest label under"** and select the parent label.Email Genie+1Sales Engagement Made Easy | Yesware+1

Q: Is there a limit to the number of labels I can create?
A: Gmail permits a substantial number of labels, so you can create as many as needed to organize your inbox effectively.

Q: Will labeling an email remove it from the inbox?
A: No, applying a label does not move the email out of the inbox. To remove it from the inbox view, you can archive the email after labeling it.

🎯 Practice Activity

1. **Create Labels:**
   - Set up labels for **Friends**, **Family**, and **Doctors** following the steps above.
2. **Apply Labels to Emails:**
   - Go through your inbox and assign the appropriate labels to existing emails.

🗄 Archiving vs. Deleting Emails

(Understanding the Differences and Best Practices for Email Management)

Effectively managing your email involves making informed decisions about whether to archive or delete messages. Both actions serve to declutter your inbox but have distinct outcomes and implications. This section will provide an in-depth understanding of archiving and deleting emails, their differences, and best practices to help you maintain an organized and efficient email system.

😊 *What Does It Mean to Archive an Email?*

Archiving an email removes it from your inbox without permanently deleting it. The message is typically moved to a designated **Archive** folder or, in services like Gmail, to the **All Mail** section. This action helps keep your inbox tidy while retaining the email for future reference.Microsoft Support+1Patrina+1Patrina

Key Characteristics of Archiving:

- **Retention:** Archived emails are preserved indefinitely until you choose to delete them.Microsoft Support+2Patrina+2Jatheon Technologies Inc.+2
- **Accessibility:** You can retrieve archived emails through the search function or by navigating to the Archive/All Mail folder.Patrina+1Microsoft Support+1
- **Inbox Management:** Archiving helps declutter your inbox without losing important information.Stony Brook IT+1Apple Support Community+1

Analogy: Think of archiving as moving documents from your desk into a filing cabinet. They're out of sight but can be accessed whenever needed.Jatheon Technologies Inc.

What Does It Mean to Delete an Email?

Deleting an email removes it from your inbox and places it in the **Trash** or **Deleted Items** folder. After a certain period (commonly 30 days), emails in the trash are permanently erased.

Key Characteristics of Deleting:

- **Temporary Storage:** Deleted emails remain in the trash for a limited time before permanent removal.
- **Permanent Removal:** Once emails are purged from the trash, they cannot be recovered.
- **Storage Management:** Deleting unnecessary emails can free up storage space in your email account.Patrina

Analogy: Deleting emails is akin to throwing away unwanted papers. They remain in the trash bin for a while before being taken out permanently.

 ## Key Differences Between Archiving and Deleting

Aspect	Archiving	Deleting
Purpose	Retain emails for future reference	Remove emails that are no longer needed
Location	Moved to Archive/All Mail folder	Moved to Trash/Deleted Items folder
Retrievability	Easily retrievable anytime	Permanently removed after a set period
Impact on Storage	Does not free up storage space	Frees up storage space upon permanent deletion

📧 When to Archive vs. When to Delete

Consider Archiving When:

- **Reference Needs:** The email contains information you might need later, such as receipts, important communications, or documentation.
- **Uncertain Importance:** You're unsure whether you'll need the email in the future but prefer to keep it just in case.
- **Inbox Decluttering:** You want to keep your inbox organized without losing potentially valuable emails.

Consider Deleting When:

- **Irrelevance:** The email is no longer relevant or useful, such as outdated promotions or spam.
- **Confidentiality:** The email contains sensitive information that should not be retained.
- **Storage Management:** You need to free up space in your email account by removing unnecessary messages.LinkedIn

🛠️ Best Practices for Email Management

1. **Regular Review:** Periodically assess your inbox to decide which emails to archive or delete.
2. **Use Folders/Labels:** Organize archived emails into specific folders or labels for easier retrieval.
3. **Set Retention Policies:** Establish personal guidelines for how long to keep certain types of emails.
4. **Be Cautious with Deletion:** Only delete emails when you're certain they're no longer needed, as recovery might not be possible after permanent deletion.
5. **Leverage Search Functions:** Utilize your email service's search capabilities to locate archived emails quickly.

☹ Common Questions

Q: Can I retrieve a deleted email?
A: Yes, but only if it's still in the Trash/Deleted Items folder. Once it's permanently deleted, recovery is typically not possible.

Q: Does archiving free up storage space?
A: No, archiving retains the email in your account. To free up space, you need to delete emails permanently.Patrina

Q: How long do emails stay in the trash?
A: Most email services keep deleted emails in the trash for about 30 days before permanent deletion.

◎ Practice Activity

1. **Identify Emails to Archive:**
   o Go through your inbox and select emails that contain important information you might need later.Patrina
   o Archive these emails using your email service's archive function.
2. **Identify Emails to Delete:**
   o Find emails that are no longer relevant or useful.Patrina
   o Move these emails to the trash and ensure they're permanently deleted after the retention period.

Reflection: Regularly practicing archiving and deleting emails will help maintain an organized and efficient inbox.

☺ *Final Thoughts*

Understanding the differences between archiving and deleting emails is crucial for effective email management. By thoughtfully deciding which action to take, you can keep your inbox organized, retain important information, and manage your email storage effectively.

Remember, archiving is best for preserving emails you might need in the future, while deleting is suitable for removing unnecessary messages permanently. Regularly applying these practices will lead to a more streamlined and efficient email experience.

🔍 Using the Search Bar to Find Old Emails

(Mastering Gmail's Search Functionality for Efficient Email Retrieval)

Efficiently managing your emails involves not only organizing them but also being able to retrieve specific messages when needed. Gmail's robust search functionality allows you to locate old emails swiftly using various techniques and operators. This section will guide you through mastering Gmail's search bar to enhance your email management skills.

😊 *Understanding Gmail's Search Bar*

Gmail's search bar, located at the top of your inbox, functions similarly to a search engine, enabling you to find emails based on keywords, senders, dates, and more. By inputting specific queries or utilizing advanced search operators, you can narrow down your search results to locate the exact email you're seeking.Reddit

---

🛠️ *Basic Search Techniques*

1. Keyword Search:

- **Method:** Type relevant keywords or phrases related to the email content into the search bar.Clean Email+1YouTube+1
- **Example:** Searching for "project update" will display all emails containing that phrase.

2. Sender or Recipient Search:

- **Method:** Use `from:` to search for emails from a specific sender or `to:` for emails sent to a specific recipient.Mailmeteor+1Clean Email+1

- **Example:** `from:john.doe@example.com` retrieves all emails from John Doe.

3. Subject Line Search:

- **Method:** Utilize `subject:` followed by keywords to find emails with specific words in the subject line.Clean Email
- **Example:** `subject:meeting` shows emails with "meeting" in the subject.Clean Email

---

📅 Searching Emails by Date

To locate emails from a specific time frame, Gmail offers several date-based search operators:Mailmeteor

1. `before:` and `after:` Operators:

- **Method:** Search for emails sent before or after a particular date using the format `YYYY/MM/DD`.FIT Information Technology
- **Examples:**
  - `before:2023/01/01` retrieves emails sent before January 1, 2023.Clean Email
  - `after:2023/01/01` retrieves emails sent after January 1, 2023.

2. `older_than:` and `newer_than:` Operators:

- **Method:** Find emails older or newer than a specific time frame using `d` for days, `m` for months, and `y` for years.
- **Examples:**
  - `older_than:1y` retrieves emails older than one year.FIT Information Technology+2Clean Email+2Mailmeteor+2
  - `newer_than:7d` retrieves emails from the past week.

3. Combining Date Operators:

- **Method:** Combine `before:` and `after:` to search within a date range.
- **Example:** `after:2023/01/01 before:2023/12/31` retrieves emails sent in 2023. Clean Email+2FIT Information Technology+2Google Help+2

💼 Advanced Search Operators

Gmail provides a variety of operators to refine your searches further:Clean Email+1FIT Information Technology+1

- `has:attachment`: Find emails with attachments.AP News
  - *Example:* `has:attachment project` retrieves emails containing the word "project" with attachments.
- `is:important`: Locate emails marked as important.Clean Email+1Wikipedia+1
  - *Example:* `is:important` shows all emails marked important.Clean Email
- `label:`: Search within a specific label.
  - *Example:* `label:work` retrieves emails under the "work" label.Clean Email
- `in:`: Search within specific folders like Inbox, Sent, Spam, etc.
  - *Example:* `in:sent` shows emails in the Sent folder.
- `filename:`: Find emails with a specific attachment name or type.
  - *Example:* `filename:report.pdf` retrieves emails with an attachment named "report.pdf".

🎲 Using Gmail's Advanced Search Interface

For users who prefer a graphical interface over typing operators:

1. **Access Advanced Search:**
   - Click the **filter icon** (three horizontal lines) on the right side of the search bar.
2. **Input Search Criteria:**
   - Fill in fields like **From, To, Subject, Has the words, Doesn't have, Size**, and **Date within**.
3. **Execute Search:**
   - After entering the desired criteria, click **Search** to view results.Clean Email

📱 Searching for Old Emails on Mobile Devices

Gmail's mobile app also supports advanced search functionalities:

1. **Open Gmail App:**
   - Launch the Gmail app on your smartphone or tablet.
2. **Access Search Bar:**
   - Tap on the **search bar** at the top.
3. **Enter Search Operators:**
   - Input operators like `before:`, `after:`, `from:`, etc., to refine your search.FIT Information Technology
4. **Use Built-in Filters:**
   - After typing, built-in filters may appear below the search bar to help narrow down results.

💬 Common Questions

Q: Can I search for emails within a specific label?
A: Yes, use the `label:` operator followed by the label name. For example, `label:work` searches within the "work" label.

Q: How do I find emails with attachments from a specific person?

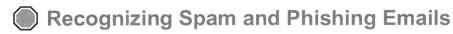 Recognizing Spam and Phishing Emails

(Identifying and Avoiding Malicious Communications)

Spam and phishing emails are prevalent threats designed to deceive recipients into divulging personal information or installing malicious software. Recognizing their characteristics is the first step toward protection.

Common Indicators of Phishing Emails:

- **Generic Greetings:** Phrases like "Dear Customer" or "Hello User" instead of your name.
- **Urgent Requests:** Messages that pressure you to act swiftly, such as claiming immediate action is required to secure your account. Microsoft Support
- **Suspicious Links:** Hyperlinks that, when hovered over, display URLs differing from the purported sender's domain. CrowdStrike
- **Unsolicited Attachments:** Unexpected files encouraging you to download, which may contain malware.NCSC
- **Requests for Sensitive Information:** Emails asking for passwords, Social Security numbers, or financial details.

Best Practices to Avoid Phishing Scams:

- **Verify Sender Information:** Examine the sender's email address for authenticity.
- **Be Cautious with Links and Attachments:** Avoid clicking on unknown links or downloading attachments from untrusted sources.
- **Use Security Software:** Employ reputable antivirus programs to detect and block malicious content.
- **Stay Informed:** Educate yourself about common phishing tactics and remain vigilant.

What to Do With Suspicious Emails

(Steps to Take When Encountering Potential Threats)

Encountering a suspicious email requires prompt and careful action to mitigate potential risks.

Recommended Actions:

1. **Do Not Interact:** Avoid clicking links, downloading attachments, or replying to the email.The Sun
2. **Verify the Source:** Contact the purported sender through official channels to confirm the email's legitimacy.
3. **Report the Email:** Use your email provider's reporting tools to flag the message as phishing or spam.
4. **Delete the Email:** Remove the suspicious email from your inbox to prevent accidental interaction.
5. **Monitor Your Accounts:** Regularly check your financial and personal accounts for unauthorized activity.

🔒 Setting a Strong Password

(Creating and Managing Secure Passwords for Your Accounts)

A strong password is a critical defense against unauthorized access to your email and other online accounts.

Characteristics of a Strong Password:

- **Length:** Aim for at least 12 characters.
- **Complexity:** Use a mix of uppercase and lowercase letters, numbers, and special characters.
- **Unpredictability:** Avoid common words, phrases, or easily guessable patterns.
- **Uniqueness:** Create different passwords for each of your online accounts.

Tips for Managing Passwords:

- **Use a Password Manager:** Securely store and generate complex passwords.
- **Regularly Update Passwords:** Change your passwords periodically and immediately if you suspect a breach.
- **Enable Account Recovery Options:** Set up security questions or backup email addresses to recover accounts if needed.

Enabling 2-Step Verification

(Adding an Extra Layer of Security to Your Accounts)

Two-step verification (2SV), also known as two-factor authentication (2FA), enhances account security by requiring two forms of identification.

Benefits of 2SV:

- **Enhanced Security:** Even if your password is compromised, unauthorized access is prevented without the second factor.
- **Reduced Risk of Phishing:** Phishing attempts are less effective against accounts with 2SV enabled.

How 2SV Works:

1. **Something You Know:** Your password.
2. **Something You Have:** A code sent to your phone, generated by an authenticator app, or a hardware security key. Microsoft Support

Setting Up 2SV:

- **Access Account Settings:** Navigate to the security settings of your email provider.
- **Enable 2SV:** Follow the prompts to activate and choose your preferred second factor method.
- **Complete Setup:** Verify the setup by entering codes sent to your chosen method. Reddit+1Google Help+1

Reporting Scams

(Taking Action Against Fraudulent Activities)

Reporting scams contributes to broader efforts to combat cybercrime and protect others.

How to Report Scams:

- **Email Provider:** Use the reporting tools provided by your email service to flag phishing or spam emails.
- **Government Agencies:** In the U.S., report to the Federal Trade Commission (FTC); in other countries, contact appropriate consumer protection agencies.
- **Organizations Affected:** Notify entities impersonated in scams, such as banks or online services.

Information to Provide When Reporting:

- **Email Content:** Include the full text of the suspicious email.
- **Sender Details:** Provide the sender's email address and any other relevant information.
- **Your Actions:** Describe any steps you've taken in response to the email.

Chapter 6: Customizing Gmail for Your Comfort

Adjusting Font Size and Layout

(Personalizing Your Email Experience for Enhanced Readability and Aesthetics)

Customizing the font size and layout in your emails can significantly enhance readability and convey your messages more effectively. Gmail offers a variety of options to personalize your email composition experience.

Changing the Default Font Size and Style in Gmail

1. Accessing Gmail Settings:

- **Step 1:** Open Gmail and click on the ⚙️ **Gear icon** located in the top right corner of your inbox.
- **Step 2:** From the dropdown menu, select **"See all settings"** to access the full settings menu.

2. Modifying Default Text Style:

- **Step 1:** In the settings menu, ensure you're on the **General** tab.
- **Step 2:** Scroll down to the **"Default text style"** section.
- **Step 3:** Here, you can customize:
    - **Font:** Choose from a variety of fonts to set your default.
    - **Size:** Select the desired font size (Small, Normal, Large, Huge).
    - **Text Color:** Pick a color that suits your preference.
    - **Highlight Color:** Set a background color for your text if desired.
- **Step 4:** After making your selections, scroll to the bottom and click **"Save Changes"** to apply them.

Note: These changes will apply to all new emails you compose.

Using the Formatting Toolbar for Individual Emails

For emails requiring unique formatting:

1. **Compose a New Email:**
   - Click on the **"Compose"** button to start a new email.
2. **Highlight Text to Format:**
   - Type your message and highlight the text you wish to format.
3. **Utilize the Formatting Toolbar:**
   - Click on the **"A"** icon with a color palette beneath it to reveal the formatting options, including:
     - **Font Style:** Select from available fonts.
     - **Font Size:** Choose from predefined sizes or set a custom size.
     - **Text Color:** Apply color to your text.
     - **Highlight Color:** Add background color to your text.
     - **Bold, Italic, Underline:** Emphasize your text as needed.
     - **Alignment:** Set text alignment (left, center, right).
     - **Numbered and Bulleted Lists:** Organize content effectively.
     - **Indentation:** Adjust text indentation for better structure.

Adjusting Email Layout for Optimal Viewing

Gmail provides options to modify the layout of your inbox and emails for a personalized experience:

1. Changing Inbox Density:

- **Step 1:** Click on the ⚙ **Gear icon** and select **"See all settings"**.
- **Step 2:** In the **General** tab, locate the **"Density"** section.
- **Step 3:** Choose from the following options:

- - **Default:** Standard spacing between emails.Campaign Monitor
  - **Comfortable:** More space between emails for easier reading.
  - **Compact:** Less space between emails to view more messages at once.
- **Step 4:** After selecting your preferred density, scroll down and click **"Save Changes"**.

2. Enabling or Disabling the Reading Pane:

The reading pane allows you to preview emails without opening them fully.

- **Step 1:** Click on the ⚙ **Gear icon** and select **"See all settings"**.
- **Step 2:** Navigate to the **"Reading pane"** tab.
- **Step 3:** Choose your preferred setting:
  - **No split:** Disable the reading pane.
  - **Vertical split:** Preview emails on the right side of your inbox.
  - **Horizontal split:** Preview emails below your inbox.
- **Step 4:** Click **"Save Changes"** to apply your selection.

Note: The reading pane feature may not be available in all Gmail versions or may require additional configuration.

Tips for Effective Email Formatting

- **Consistency:** Use consistent fonts and sizes to maintain a professional appearance.
- **Simplicity:** Avoid excessive formatting that can distract from your message.
- **Accessibility:** Ensure font sizes are readable on various devices, considering recipients who may have visual impairments.
- **Testing:** Send test emails to yourself to preview how your formatting appears to recipients.

By customizing your email's font size and layout, you can enhance readability and ensure your messages convey the intended tone and clarity.

📫 Adding an Email Signature in Gmail

Have you ever noticed how some people have their name, phone number, or a little note appear automatically at the bottom of their emails? 🗨 That's called an **email signature**, and it's a simple, helpful way to make your emails look more personal and professional.

Think of it as the modern-day version of signing off a letter with your name — only with Gmail, it can do it for you automatically every single time. ✏️🗄

📜 *What is an Email Signature?*

An email signature is a block of text (and sometimes images or links) that shows up at the end of your email messages. It might include:

- Your full name 👤
- Your phone number 📞
- A favorite quote or greeting 💬
- Your address or website (if applicable) 🌐
- Even a small image or logo 🖼

Once it's set up, Gmail will add it to the end of every email you send — no need to type it each time!

🕐 *How to Add an Email Signature (on Computer)*

Let's go through it slowly, step-by-step. Ready? Here we go! 🚀

Step 1: Open your Gmail inbox by going to mail.google.com 🖥

Step 2: In the top-right corner, click the ⚙️ **Settings icon** (it looks like a little gear).

Step 3: Click **"See all settings"** from the dropdown menu.

Step 4: You'll be taken to a new page with tabs. Make sure you're in the **"General"** tab.

Step 5: Scroll down until you find the section called **"Signature."** 🖊️

Step 6: Click **"Create new"**, then give your signature a name (this can be anything, like "My Main Signature").

Step 7: A box will appear where you can type your signature.

👉 Here's a simple example:

```
nginx
CopyEdit
Warm regards,
Susan Smith
555-123-4567
Your friendly neighborhood grandma  😊
```

Step 8: You can use the toolbar above the box to:

- Make text bold or colorful 🔤 🎨
- Add a photo or logo 🖼️
- Insert a web link 🌐

Step 9: Scroll down and look for the setting that says:
"Signature defaults" ⤷ Choose your new signature for both new emails and replies/forwards.

Step 10: Scroll all the way to the bottom and click **"Save Changes"** 💾

🎉 Done! From now on, your signature will show up at the bottom of your emails automatically.

📱 *How to Add a Signature in the Gmail App (Mobile Devices)*

Want to do it on your phone or tablet? No problem!

Step 1: Open the **Gmail app** on your device.

Step 2: Tap the ☰ **three-line menu** in the top-left corner.

Step 3: Scroll down and tap **"Settings."**

Step 4: Choose the Gmail account you want to add the signature to.

Step 5: Scroll down and tap **"Mobile Signature."**
Step 6: Type your signature in the box and tap **"OK."**

📌 **Note:** Mobile signatures can only be plain text — no colors or images — but it still does the trick!

💡 *Tips for Seniors When Creating a Signature*

- **Keep it simple.** Just your name and phone number is often enough.
- **Use larger text** if you have vision issues — on desktop, you can increase font size.
- **Don't share sensitive info** like passwords or personal addresses unless absolutely necessary.

💬 *Try This Interactive Exercise!*

✏️ On a piece of paper or in a notepad app, write your ideal email signature. Try including:

- Your name
- A contact number
- A short message or quote you love

Now, practice typing it into the Gmail signature box using the steps above. It's your personal stamp! 👣

📪 Adding an Email Signature in Gmail

Have you ever noticed how some people have their name, phone number, or a little note appear automatically at the bottom of their emails? ✉️ That's called an **email signature**, and it's a simple, helpful way to make your emails look more personal and professional.

Think of it as the modern-day version of signing off a letter with your name — only with Gmail, it can do it for you automatically every single time. ✏️📩

📜 *What is an Email Signature?*

An email signature is a block of text (and sometimes images or links) that shows up at the end of your email messages. It might include:

- Your full name 👤
- Your phone number 📞
- A favorite quote or greeting 💬
- Your address or website (if applicable) 🌐
- Even a small image or logo 🖼️

Once it's set up, Gmail will add it to the end of every email you send — no need to type it each time!

🧭 *How to Add an Email Signature (on Computer)*

Let's go through it slowly, step-by-step. Ready? Here we go! 🚀

Step 1: Open your Gmail inbox by going to mail.google.com 🖥️
Step 2: In the top-right corner, click the ⚙️ **Settings icon** (it looks like a little gear).
Step 3: Click **"See all settings"** from the dropdown menu.

Step 4: You'll be taken to a new page with tabs. Make sure you're in the **"General"** tab.

Step 5: Scroll down until you find the section called **"Signature."** 🖊

Step 6: Click **"Create new"**, then give your signature a name (this can be anything, like "My Main Signature").

Step 7: A box will appear where you can type your signature.

👉 Here's a simple example:

```
nginx
CopyEdit
Warm regards,
Susan Smith
555-123-4567
Your friendly neighborhood grandma 😊
```

Step 8: You can use the toolbar above the box to:

- Make text bold or colorful 🔤 🎨
- Add a photo or logo 🖼
- Insert a web link 🌐

Step 9: Scroll down and look for the setting that says:

"Signature defaults" → Choose your new signature for both new emails and replies/forwards.

Step 10: Scroll all the way to the bottom and click **"Save Changes"** 💾

🎉 Done! From now on, your signature will show up at the bottom of your emails automatically.

📱 *How to Add a Signature in the Gmail App (Mobile Devices)*

Want to do it on your phone or tablet? No problem!

Step 1: Open the **Gmail app** on your device.

Step 2: Tap the ☰ **three-line menu** in the top-left corner.

Step 3: Scroll down and tap **"Settings."**

Step 4: Choose the Gmail account you want to add the signature to.

Step 5: Scroll down and tap **"Mobile Signature."**

Step 6: Type your signature in the box and tap **"OK."**

📌 **Note:** Mobile signatures can only be plain text — no colors or images — but it still does the trick!

💡 *Tips for Seniors When Creating a Signature*

- **Keep it simple.** Just your name and phone number is often enough.
- **Use larger text** if you have vision issues — on desktop, you can increase font size.
- **Don't share sensitive info** like passwords or personal addresses unless absolutely necessary.

💬 *Try This Interactive Exercise!*

✏️ On a piece of paper or in a notepad app, write your ideal email signature. Try including:

- Your name
- A contact number
- A short message or quote you love

Now, practice typing it into the Gmail signature box using the steps above. It's your personal stamp! 👣

🔔 Notifications: Turning Alerts On or Off

Have you ever missed an important email because you didn't hear a sound or see a message pop up? Or maybe your phone keeps buzzing at night with email alerts when you're trying to sleep? 😵‍💫📱

That's where **notifications** come in — and the good news is, you can **turn them on or off**, and even **choose how and when** Gmail notifies you!

💭 *What Are Gmail Notifications?*

Gmail notifications are little alerts (sounds, banners, or pop-ups) that let you know when a new email arrives. You might see them:

- On your **computer screen** 🖥️
- On your **phone or tablet** 📱
- As a **sound** or **vibration**

These alerts are helpful — especially if you're expecting an important message from your doctor, family member, or grandchild! But too many can be distracting.

The good news? You're in charge!

📱 How to Manage Notifications on Your Phone or Tablet

Let's walk through the steps on your mobile device:

✅ *To Turn ON Notifications:*

Step 1: Open the **Gmail app**
Step 2: Tap the ☰ **three-line menu** in the top-left corner
Step 3: Scroll down and tap **"Settings"**
Step 4: Choose the email account you want to adjust
Step 5: Tap **"Notifications"**
Step 6: Select **"All"** to get notified for every new email
☞ You'll hear a sound or see a message pop up when a new email arrives!

🔔 *To Turn OFF Notifications:*

Follow the same steps above, but in **Step 6**, choose **"None"**

This means you'll still get your emails, but Gmail won't bother you with alerts. Perfect for quiet evenings or peaceful naps. 😌 🌙

🖥️ How to Manage Notifications on Your Computer (Web Browser)

Let's do it on your computer now:

Step 1: Open Gmail on your browser (go to mail.google.com)
Step 2: Click the ⚙️ **Settings icon** in the top right
Step 3: Click **"See all settings"**
Step 4: Scroll down under the **"General" tab**

Step 5: Look for the section labeled **"Desktop Notifications"**
Step 6: Choose one of the following:

- **"New mail notifications on"** – get notified for all incoming emails 🖥
- **"Important mail notifications on"** – only get notified for emails Gmail thinks are important (like family, appointments, etc.)
- **"Mail notifications off"** – no pop-ups or alerts

Step 7: Click **"Save Changes"** at the bottom 🖱 💾

✅ **Tip:** Your browser may ask if Gmail is allowed to show notifications. Click **"Allow"** if you want alerts.

🙂💬 *Interactive Reflection:*

Ask yourself these questions:

- Do I want to know *immediately* when someone sends me an email?
- Or would I rather *check on my own time* without being interrupted?

You're the boss of your inbox! 👑

If you're not sure, try turning them ON during the day and OFF in the evening — experiment and see what works best for your lifestyle.

🔔 *Bonus Tip: Customize Sounds and Vibration!*

On mobile, go back into Gmail Settings ⬅ tap **"Inbox sound & vibrate"**
You can pick a special sound, adjust vibration, or silence it altogether 🎵 🔊

This way, you'll know when it's an email and not a random app bothering you!

🎉 You Did It!

You've now learned how to manage your Gmail notifications like a pro. Whether you want peace and quiet or to stay in the loop, Gmail gives you control.

Chapter 7: Gmail on Mobile Devices

Installing the Gmail App (Android/iPhone)

📱 *How to Install Gmail on an iPhone or iPad (iOS)*

f you're using an iPhone or iPad, follow these steps:

☑ **Step-by-step instructions:**

1. Tap on the **App Store icon** (it looks like a blue "A" made of popsicle sticks)
2. Tap the **search** icon (magnifying glass) in the bottom-right corner
3. Type **"Gmail"** into the search bar
4. Find the app called **Gmail – Email by Google**
5. Tap the **Get** button (you may need to enter your Apple ID password or use Face ID/Touch ID)
6. Wait for the download to finish ⌛
7. Tap **Open**, or go to your home screen and tap the Gmail icon to begin 📫

💡 *Helpful Tips:*

- The Gmail app is **completely free** 🎁
- You only need to install it once — updates happen automatically!
- If it's already installed (some Android devices come with it), just **open it** and sign in

---

😊💬 *Let's Reflect:*

- Have you ever installed an app before?
- Try doing it now! You can always uninstall if you change your mind.

- If you're nervous, ask a family member or friend to walk through it with you — or better yet, do it together as a fun activity! 👨‍👩‍👧

🎉 You're All Set!

Once the app is installed, you're ready to log in and start sending and receiving emails from anywhere.

Let me know when you're ready to move on to the next subchapter: **Signing In and Using Gmail on Phones or Tablets**! 📱✉️

📱 Signing In and Using Gmail on Phones or Tablets

Now that you've installed the Gmail app (woohoo! 🎉), it's time to **sign in** and start using it on your phone or tablet. This step is all about **unlocking your inbox on the go**, so you can read and reply to messages wherever you are — from the couch, the park, or even the grocery store! 🛒 🖥️

🍞 *How to Sign In to the Gmail App*

Whether you're on Android or iPhone, the process is mostly the same. Let's walk through it step-by-step:

✅ *Step-by-Step Sign-In Guide:*

1. **Open the Gmail app** by tapping the red and white envelope icon 🔲
2. Tap **"Sign in"** or **"Add account"** if it's your first time
3. Type your **Google email address** (example: **grandma.jane@gmail.com**) and tap **Next**
4. Enter your **password** 🖱️🔒 (don't worry if you forget — there's a "Forgot password?" link to help!)
5. Tap **Next** again
6. If you have **2-step verification** turned on (which we recommend for security 🛡️), you'll be asked to verify using a code or your phone — just follow the instructions
7. Ta-da! You're in! 😺 Your inbox should now be visible!

🖼️ *What You'll See After Signing In*

Once you're signed in, you'll land on the **Inbox screen**. Here's a quick rundown:

- **Inbox (Primary Tab)**: This is where most of your emails will appear — messages from family, friends, and services you use
- **Social and Promotions Tabs**: These are extra folders for emails from Facebook, newsletters, or shopping deals 🛍️ (you can ignore them or explore them later)
- **Top Menu Bar**: Contains the magnifying glass (search), three lines (menu), and other icons

110

It might look small at first, but **don't be intimidated!** Zooming in, adjusting font sizes, or just poking around helps you feel more comfortable 😊

📫 *How to Use Gmail on Your Device*

Once you're inside Gmail, you can:

- **Read messages**: Just tap one and it will open. Scroll up and down to read it fully 📖
- **Delete or archive**: Tap the little trash can 🗑 or box with an arrow 🗄 at the top
- **Reply**: Look for the curved arrow or tap the three dots for more options
- **Check older emails**: Scroll down in your inbox or use the search bar 🔍

And the best part? Gmail **automatically updates** your inbox, so you don't need to refresh it like a website. New messages will just pop up on their own! 🔔

😊💬 *Interactive Pause: Let's Try It Together!*

➡️ **Have your phone in your hand?** Try signing in right now!

➡️ **Don't have your password?** No problem — hit that "Forgot password?" and follow the steps. You've got this! 💪

➡️ **Ask for help** if needed. Tech-savvy grandkids or neighbors love showing off their skills 😊

💡 *Pro Tips:*

- **Stay signed in** so you don't have to enter your info every time
- If you use multiple Google accounts, you can add them all and switch between them easily 🔄
- Use the **Settings** option in the app (tap your profile photo in the corner) to customize your experience

---

🎉 **Way to go!** Now you're signed in and ready to roll! You've unlocked the gateway to staying in touch anytime, anywhere — how amazing is that? ✨

📷 Sending Photos from Your Phone

One of the most delightful things about Gmail is how easy it is to send a photo 📷 — whether it's a cute grandkid moment, your beautiful garden blooms 🌺, or even a picture of that recipe you want to share. In this subchapter, we'll walk through **how to send photos from your phone using the Gmail app**, step-by-step!

🕐 *Why Would You Send Photos via Gmail?*

Before diving into the how-to, let's quickly cover the **why**:

- You want to **share memories** with family and friends 💜
- You need to send a picture of **important documents** 📄
- You'd like to share something exciting — like your artwork, a home project, or even a funny sign you saw 😄

Email is a safe, direct, and easy way to do all of this.

📤 *How to Attach a Photo to an Email*

Ready to send your first photo through Gmail on your phone? Follow along — you can even try it as we go! 👇

✅ Step-by-Step Guide (Android & iPhone):

1. **Open the Gmail app**
   Tap the red and white envelope icon on your home screen
2. **Tap the pencil icon** 📝
   This is usually at the bottom-right — it opens a **new email**
3. **Enter the recipient's email**
   For example, type in: **susan@example.com**
4. **Type your message**
   Say something like: *"Hi Susan! Here's the photo I mentioned 😊"*
5. **Tap the paperclip 📎 or attach icon**
   This will open your **file or photo gallery**

6. **Choose "Attach file" or "Insert from Photos"**
   On Android: You may see both options
   On iPhone: It might say "Photo Library" or "Attach File"
7. **Select the photo you want to send**
   Tap on it — you'll see it load into your email
8. **Double-check everything**
   Make sure the photo is attached and your message looks good
9. **Tap Send (the paper airplane icon)** 🛫
   That's it! Off it goes 🎊

📁 *Tips for Sending Photos*

- You can attach **more than one photo** at a time — just repeat the attach step!
- If the photo file is large, Gmail might automatically upload it via **Google Drive** — this is still totally fine, and the recipient can easily open it ✅
- Keep your email polite and warm — a simple greeting and closing adds a nice touch 🗨️😊

🛠️ *Troubleshooting Common Issues:*

- **Can't find the paperclip?** Look for three dots (⋮) — tap it to find more options
- **Photo too large?** Try sending it in lower resolution (your gallery app may offer that)
- **Accidentally added the wrong photo?** Just tap the "X" on the photo to remove it and reattach the correct one

---

🎯 *Interactive Practice Time!*

Give it a try now! 📱

1. Open Gmail
2. Start a new email
3. Attach a fun or recent photo

4. Send it to someone you trust — a friend, a family member, or even yourself for practice!

They'll love hearing from you, and you'll love seeing how easy it is.

✵ Final Thoughts

Sending photos through Gmail is a **wonderful way to stay connected** — especially when you can't be there in person. Whether it's a holiday memory or a quick snapshot of your garden, it brings a smile to someone's face 😊

✉📱 Managing Emails on the Go

Whether you're sipping tea in your garden 🌿, waiting at the doctor's office 🏥, or enjoying a relaxing afternoon on the porch 🌼 — you can check, read, and manage your Gmail right from your phone or tablet. This is called *emailing on the go*, and it makes staying connected so much easier!

In this subchapter, you'll learn how to **manage your inbox**, organize messages, and stay in control — all from your mobile device. Let's get started! 🧍📤

🌐 *What Does "Managing Emails" Mean?*

Managing emails simply means:

- Reading and replying to messages 📬
- Deleting, archiving, or moving emails to folders 📁
- Keeping your inbox neat and easy to use 🧹
- Making sure you don't miss important updates 🔔

When you manage emails well — even on the go — your digital life becomes a lot simpler and stress-free 🐧📱

🧭 *Navigating the Gmail App*

Once you open the Gmail app on your phone, you'll be greeted by your **Inbox** — this is where all your new emails land. Here's what you'll see and can do:

📇 *Main Screen Features:*

- **Search bar** 🔍 – Find emails quickly
- **Compose button** 📝 – Write a new email
- **Email list** 📄 – Tap on any email to read
- **Three-line menu (☰)** – Access other folders like Sent, Spam, Drafts, etc.
- **Profile picture/icon** (top right) – Manage accounts if you have more than one

Take a moment to open your app and follow along. You'll feel like a pro in no time!

🖌 *Cleaning Up: Deleting and Archiving*

Let's learn how to tidy up your inbox:

🗑 *To Delete an Email:*

1. Tap and hold the email you want to delete
2. A trash can icon will appear at the top — tap it
3. Poof! It's gone from your inbox (but stored in "Trash" for 30 days in case you change your mind)

📦 *To Archive an Email:*

1. Swipe the email left or right 🔲 🔲
2. That's it! It's saved in "All Mail" but removed from your inbox

😕 What's the difference?

- **Delete** = removes it completely after 30 days
- **Archive** = keeps it, just hides it from your main inbox

🔄 *Replying and Forwarding*

You can quickly respond to messages on the go too!

To Reply:

1. Open the email 📧
2. Tap the **Reply arrow** 🔄 at the bottom
3. Type your message and tap **Send** (✈)

To Forward:

1. Tap the three dots (⋮) in the top corner of the email

117

2. Choose **Forward**
3. Add the new recipient, message, and hit **Send**

Super handy when sharing important info like appointment times, family updates, or even funny jokes 😄

📁 *Moving Emails to Folders/Labels*

Want to sort your emails? Here's how:

1. Tap and hold the email
2. Tap the three-dot menu (⋮)
3. Select **Move to** or **Label**
4. Pick your folder like "Family" or "Health"

Easy peasy! 🗂 Organizing your inbox helps you **find what you need, when you need it.**

📱 *Check Your Email Anytime, Anywhere!*

The best part? You can:

*   Read your emails while **waiting in line**
*   Send quick replies while **relaxing at home**
*   Archive or delete while **sitting on the bus**

You're always connected, and always in control! 🧑📱

🎯 *Practice Time!*

Here's a fun mini-mission you can try today:

1. Open Gmail on your phone
2. Find an email you no longer need — delete it 🗑
3. Open another one — archive it

4. Reply to a message — even just to say "Thanks!" 🙏
5. Try moving a message into a folder like "Friends" or "Doctors"

✅ Every step you take makes you more confident and capable!

🎇 Final Thoughts

Managing your Gmail on the go puts **freedom and flexibility** right at your fingertips 🎇 Whether you're staying in touch with loved ones or keeping up with important updates, you're now equipped to do it *anytime, anywhere.* 📭📱

Chapter 8: Contacts and Groups

🖫 Adding and Saving New Contacts

When you start using Gmail, one of the most important things is building your **contacts list**. This allows you to quickly and easily send emails to friends, family, colleagues, and others. But don't worry — adding new contacts is quick and easy!

🧭 *Why Add Contacts?*

By adding a contact, Gmail remembers that person's name and email address, so you don't have to type their email every time. It's a time-saver, and it also helps you avoid errors (like sending emails to the wrong address!). Gmail even suggests contacts when you start typing, making everything faster.

📝 *How to Add a New Contact*

Here's how to add a contact to your Gmail account from your phone:

1. **Open the Gmail App** 📱
   Tap the Gmail icon to open the app and go to your Inbox.
2. **Tap the Menu Icon** ☰ (three horizontal lines)
   This is in the upper-left corner of the screen.
3. **Select "Contacts"**
   You'll see this option near the bottom of the menu. Tap it to open your Contacts list.
4. **Add a New Contact** ✚
   Tap the "+" symbol or **"Create Contact"** option, usually at the bottom-right of the screen.
5. **Enter the Contact Details**
   Type in their **name**, **email address**, and any other info you want to include (like phone number, address, etc.). Don't forget to hit "Save" after you're done.

120

6. **Done!** 🎉
   Your contact is now saved, and the next time you need to send an email, Gmail will auto-suggest them when you start typing their name.

🎯 *Pro Tip*

You can add a picture to your contact if you'd like! Just tap the camera icon when editing the contact to upload a photo of them. It makes your contacts list feel more personal and organized! 😊 📷

✄ Editing or Deleting Contacts

Sometimes, we need to update a contact's information — maybe their phone number changed, or they got a new email address. Or perhaps you no longer need someone's details in your contact list (no offense 😆). Luckily, Gmail makes it easy to **edit** or **delete** contacts.

🧭 *Editing a Contact*

Here's how to change a contact's details:

1. **Open the Contacts App**
   Tap the **three-line menu** ☰ in Gmail and select **Contacts**.
2. **Find the Contact**
   Scroll through your list or use the search bar to find the contact you need to edit.
3. **Select the Contact**
   Tap on their name to open their details.
4. **Tap the Pencil Icon** 🖊
   This icon is usually in the top-right corner and allows you to **edit** the contact.
5. **Make Your Changes**
   Update the contact's name, email address, phone number, or any other information.
6. **Save the Changes** ✅
   Don't forget to tap **Save** when you're finished!

🗑 *Deleting a Contact*

If you want to remove a contact, here's how:

1. Follow steps 1 to 3 from above to find and open the contact.
2. Tap the **three dots** (⋮) in the top-right corner.
3. Select **Delete** from the dropdown menu.
4. Confirm that you want to delete the contact, and voilà — they're gone!

🔔 **Important Reminder:** Deleting a contact will **remove them from your Gmail address book** entirely. However, it doesn't delete any emails you've exchanged with them.

👥 Creating Contact Groups (for Family, Church, Clubs, etc.)

One of the coolest features in Gmail is the ability to organize your contacts into **groups**. This is perfect for sending emails to a specific set of people, like your family, your church group, or even a book club 📚. Instead of typing everyone's email address individually, you can just type the group name and Gmail will send your message to everyone in the group at once!

⊛ *Why Create Contact Groups?*

Creating groups saves you time and keeps your email communications organized. Some examples of groups you might create:

- **Family** — for all your loved ones 👪
- **Friends** — for your closest pals 👫
- **Work** — for colleagues or business contacts 💼
- **Club Members** — if you're part of a hobby group 🎮 or a book club 📖

Gmail even allows you to send group emails and manage your contact lists quickly and easily.

122

📝 *How to Create a Contact Group*

Follow these steps to create your very own group:

1. **Open the Contacts App**
   Go into Gmail and tap the **three-line menu** ☰, then select **Contacts**.
2. **Tap the Label Icon** 🏷
   This icon will appear once you select a contact or tap on **Create Label** (usually at the bottom). This will let you create a new group.
3. **Create a New Label**
   A pop-up will appear asking you to enter a name for the group. This is the name that will represent the group in your contact list. You can name it **"Family"**, **"Friends"**, or anything you want! Type the name and hit **Save**.
4. **Add Contacts to the Group**
   Once the label is created, you can add contacts to it:
   - Tap on the group name.
   - Select **Add Contacts**.
   - Choose the contacts you want to include in this group.
5. **Done!** 🎉
   Now you have a contact group ready to go! The next time you send an email, just start typing the group name, and Gmail will auto-complete it with all the members of the group.

🎯 *Tip for Easy Group Emailing*

When you send an email to a group, Gmail will auto-fill the email address of each person in the group. However, if you want to **hide the emails from others**, use the **BCC** (Blind Carbon Copy) field when sending a group email. This keeps everyone's email addresses private. 🛡

🎇 *Final Thoughts*

Managing your contacts in Gmail is **easy, fast, and convenient**. Whether you're adding new contacts, organizing them into groups, or keeping everything up to date, Gmail has you covered. By learning how to manage contacts and groups, you're taking a big step toward mastering Gmail and staying connected with the people who matter most! ✉

Now, you're ready to send emails to all your groups at once, save time, and never forget an important person in your life again.

Chapter 9: Troubleshooting and Help

🔑 Forgot Your Password? Here's What to Do

I t happens to all of us — we forget our password. 😬 Don't worry, though! Gmail has an easy way to help you get back into your account. Here's how you can recover your password and get back to sending those emails.

Why You Might Forget Your Password

Sometimes, passwords just slip our minds. If you've changed your password recently, used multiple devices, or haven't signed in for a while, it can be easy to forget. But don't worry, Gmail has got your back! 💪

📝 How to Reset Your Password

Follow these steps if you can't remember your Gmail password:

1. **Go to the Gmail Sign-In Page**
   Open your browser and go to Gmail. You'll see the sign-in screen.
2. **Click on "Forgot Password?"**
   Underneath the password field, you'll see the link **"Forgot password?"**. Click this to start the recovery process.
3. **Enter Your Email Address**
   You'll be asked to enter your **Gmail address** (the one you can't access). This helps Gmail locate your account.
4. **Choose a Recovery Method**
   Gmail will offer different ways to recover your account:
   - **Phone Number**: If you linked a phone number to your account, Gmail will send a verification code via text.
   - **Backup Email**: If you've set up a secondary email address, you'll receive a code there.

- ○ **Answer Security Questions**: If you've set security questions, you might need to answer them.
5. **Enter the Verification Code**
   Once you receive the code on your phone or backup email, enter it into the provided field.
6. **Create a New Password**
   Once verified, you'll be prompted to **create a new password**. Choose something strong and memorable! 🔑 💡 Make sure it's at least **8 characters**, combining letters, numbers, and symbols.
7. **Sign In**
   After resetting, you'll be able to sign in to your Gmail account using your new password. 🎉

🎯 *Pro Tip:*

Make sure you keep your new password in a secure location, like a password manager or a safe spot in your phone. 📱 🔐

⚙️ Gmail Running Slow? Quick Fixes

Is Gmail taking forever to load? 😫 Don't worry! There are simple fixes to speed things up so you can get back to emailing in no time. Here's what to do if Gmail is lagging or not working as quickly as usual.

✳️ *Common Reasons Gmail May Be Slow*

- **Poor Internet Connection** 🌐: A weak Wi-Fi or cellular signal can cause Gmail to load slowly.
- **Too Many Tabs Open** 🗔: If you have multiple tabs open in your browser, Gmail may get bogged down.
- **Outdated Browser or App** 📱: Using an old version of Gmail or your browser could slow down performance.

127

📝 Quick Fixes to Speed Things Up

1. **Check Your Internet Connection**
   First, make sure your internet connection is working. Test by opening another website to see if it's loading properly. If it's not, try reconnecting to your Wi-Fi or moving closer to your router.
2. **Close Unnecessary Tabs**
   Too many open tabs can slow down your browser. Try closing any extra tabs and keeping only Gmail open.
3. **Clear Browser Cache**
   Over time, your browser collects data that can slow things down. Here's how to clear the cache:
   - **On Chrome**: Click the three dots in the top-right corner, select **Settings**, then go to **Privacy and Security** > **Clear Browsing Data**. Choose **Cached Images and Files** and hit **Clear Data**.
4. **Update Your Browser**
   Make sure you're using the latest version of your browser. You can usually update it by going to **Settings** > **About** and checking for updates.
5. **Update the Gmail App**
   If you're using Gmail on a phone or tablet, go to the **App Store (iOS)** or **Google Play Store (Android)** and make sure you have the latest version of the Gmail app installed.

🎯 Pro Tip:

If Gmail is still slow after trying these tips, it might help to **restart your device** or **clear the cache** on your phone's Gmail app.

📞 How to Reach Google Support

Sometimes things go wrong, and you just need a little help from Google's support team. Whether you have a technical issue or need assistance, reaching out to Google Support is easy!

🕐 *Why Contact Support?*

If you've tried all the basic troubleshooting steps and your issue isn't fixed, or you have a more complex problem, Google Support is there to help.

📝 *How to Contact Google Support*

1. **Go to the Google Help Center**
   In your browser, go to the Google Help Center.
2. **Search for Your Issue**
   Use the search bar to describe your issue. Google has articles and tips that might solve your problem.
3. **Click on "Contact Us"**
   If you can't find a solution in the Help Center, scroll to the bottom and click the **"Contact Us"** button.
4. **Select Your Support Option**
   Depending on the problem, Google will offer several ways to get in touch:
   - **Chat Support** 💬: Speak with a Google representative through a live chat.
   - **Email Support** 📧: Send an email with your issue and wait for a response.
   - **Phone Support** 📞: Get a phone number to call and talk to someone directly.
5. **Describe Your Issue**
   When contacting support, be sure to give as many details as possible about your problem, including the device and browser you're using, any error messages, and what steps you've already taken to fix it.

Pro Tip:

When dealing with customer service, stay patient and calm. 📞 If you're talking to someone on the phone, take notes to ensure you don't forget anything important. 🗒️

📚 Helpful Resources for Continued Learning

Once you've got Gmail down, you might want to explore more advanced features. There are plenty of resources to help you continue learning, whether you're new to email or want to master Gmail like a pro.

🧭 Why Keep Learning?

Gmail is packed with features, and while we've covered the essentials, there's always something new to discover. These resources will help you stay on top of all the updates and tips for using Gmail effectively.

📝 Resources for Gmail Learning

1. **Google Help Center**
   You're already familiar with it! The Google Help Center is a treasure trove of articles, tips, and FAQs.
2. **Google's Official YouTube Channel** 📺
   Google's YouTube channel has tons of video tutorials. From basic tips to advanced Gmail features, you can watch and learn at your own pace.
3. **Google Workspace Training Center**
   If you want to go beyond Gmail, check out the Google Workspace Training Center for in-depth lessons on Google Docs, Sheets, and more.
4. **Online Communities and Forums**
   Join online forums like **Reddit** or **Google's product forums** to ask questions, get advice, and share tips with other Gmail users.

ⓖ *Pro Tip:*

Don't hesitate to ask questions! Online communities are full of helpful people, and the Google Help Center is constantly updated with new information. Stay curious and keep learning! ▢

✳ Final Thoughts

Troubleshooting doesn't have to be stressful! 💪 With these steps and resources, you can solve common problems like forgotten passwords, slow performance, and reaching out to Google Support. Keep these tricks handy, and you'll always feel confident using Gmail. Keep up the great work! 🎉

You Did It!

If this guide made Gmail easier for you, please leave a short review and share your experience. Your feedback helps others, just like you, feel confident online.
Thank you for being a part of the Chittah Publishing family!

www.ingramcontent.com/pod-product-compliance
Lightning Source LLC
LaVergne TN
LVHW081758050326
832903LV00027B/2003